THE POSITION OF WOMEN
IN THE U.S.S.R.

THE POSITION OF WOMEN IN THE U.S.S.R.

by

G. N. SEREBRENNIKOV

 BOOKS FOR LIBRARIES PRESS
FREEPORT, NEW YORK

HD6166
.S38

First Published 1937
Reprinted 1970

INTERNATIONAL STANDARD BOOK NUMBER:
0-8369-5585-4

LIBRARY OF CONGRESS CATALOG CARD NUMBER:
72-137384

PRINTED IN THE UNITED STATES OF AMERICA

CONTENTS

Introduction *page* 7

Chapter I. Soviet Laws on the Rights of Women and for the Protection of the Woman Worker 9

II. General Results of the Development of Women's Work in the Soviet Union 26

III. Woman as a Skilled Worker 59

IV. Women in Collectivisation 87

V. Woman in the Intellectual Professions and in Administrative Work 117

VI. Towards a Healthier Life for Women 141

VII. Cultural Growth and Social Activity among Working Women 191

VIII. Women in the National Republics 224

Conclusion 252

Appendix I. Extract from Code of Labour Laws of the U.S.S.R. 259

Appendix II. Decree on the Prohibition of Abortions, etc. (Decision of the C.E.C. and the Council of People's Commissars of the U.S.S.R.) *page* 261

INTRODUCTION

THIS BOOK IS DEDICATED to the work and general position of woman in the Soviet Union. In this field the U.S.S.R. has tremendous achievements to record—achievements that reflect the immense social reconstruction which in a historically short period of time has completely changed the entire social aspect of the country. The U.S.S.R. is the only country in the world where full equality for women has not only been proclaimed, but is also being made an actuality. Soviet woman is participating in all forms of public work, and occupies a secure and important place both in the national economic structure and in the social and cultural life of the country. She has established herself in industry and agriculture, in science and technical research, in directing production and in State administration. In a country in which but twenty years ago the overwhelming majority of the female population was illiterate, there are at present almost no illiterate women. In all schools, women study side by side with men. The whole mode of life of the Soviet woman is being changed.

And, despite all these changes, motherhood is

INTRODUCTION

flourishing. The birth-rate is constantly increasing; child mortality greatly decreasing. Soviet woman is beginning to play her full part in raising a new generation; and in doing so she is receiving the full support and protection of the State and people.

The author's aim is to throw light on the great cultural and social development of the Soviet woman, and show concretely how the principle of full equality for women—their real liberation and emancipation—is being carried out in the U.S.S.R.

The author is an investigator; and his narrative is therefore based on a statistical examination of his theme. He hopes the reader who seriously wishes to learn what is taking place with regard to women in the Soviet Union will not be dismayed by the abundance of statistical data in this book. Much space is also devoted to facts that primarily concern individual careers. But such personal records, however striking and illuminating they may be, are not so convincing as are discussions of general conditions, if only because records of another, and a contradictory, nature may exist, of which the author may not know or of which he may not choose to speak.

Only mass evidence carries with it the power of conviction. And it is in the language of mass evidence, a language of unbiased actuality, that the author speaks to the reader.

CHAPTER I

SOVIET LAWS ON THE RIGHTS OF WOMEN AND FOR THE PROTECTION OF THE WOMAN WORKER

V. I. LENIN, the organiser and leader of the Soviet State, always devoted much attention to the problems of women's life and work. He taught that the Socialist ideal, which is now in process of being realised in the Soviet Union, demands the abolition of all kinds of exploitation of man by man, and thus of all forms of social inequality, including the inequality between man and woman that exists in every society that is divided into classes.

The Soviet authorities took as their aims the conquest of woman's age-long inferiority, and the achievement of complete and real equality between her and man. These principles underlie all Soviet legislation that affects the position of women and the conditions of female labour.

In Tsarist Russia, a woman shared in the general exclusion from political rights that characterised the period, and was barred from all but the most limited civil rights. Her position was particularly humiliating in relation to her husband and family. She was, under Tsarist law, literally a slave to her husband. A married woman had no right of unrestricted movement: every time her husband changed his abode she was obliged to follow him. Her possessions were under her husband's complete control. She could go to work only with his consent. If her marriage turned out badly, she had to submit to her fate, since she had no lawful means of redress. If she left her husband, he had the right to invoke the aid of the police in searching for her. Divorce was granted only in exceptional instances; and even then it could be obtained only with extreme difficulty and after the woman had undergone humiliating formalities and had submitted to gross intrusion into her private life by judge and police. Moreover, divorce was beyond the means of any but a rich woman.

The subordinate position of women meant that the father had first rights over the children. Church marriage was the only form of union admitted by law. A woman who bore children out of lawful wedlock could neither take action against the father nor search him out. All the burden of rearing the illegitimate child fell on her.

AND FOR PROTECTION

At the very beginning of its activity, the Soviet Government abolished all marriage and family laws that were based on the enslavement of women, and created a new legal system founded on the complete equality of women in marriage and in the family. The Soviet authorities attach particular significance to the strengthening of the family and the creation of enduring and stable marital relations—ends which can only be attained on a basis of equal rights and mutual respect between husband and wife.

These principles underlie all aspects of married life in the Soviet Union. Formerly the husband was always " head of the family "; but this conception is quite foreign to Soviet life, as is exemplified in the fact that a woman is not obliged to take her husband's name after marriage. Both husband and wife have complete freedom in the choice of an occupation or profession. Possessions acquired during marriage are considered to be joint property, and any quarrel as to their division is settled by law. Possessions belonging to either party before marriage remain the separate property of each. Thus the mercenary motive for marriage has been destroyed in the Soviet Union. Marriages for dowry, so frequent in Tsarist Russia and in the overwhelming majority of countries even to-day, are now impossible in the U.S.S.R. Soviet legislation has established marriage by civil registration. Church marriage is not prohibited by law; but it is regarded as the " private business of the parties to marriage " whether a religious ceremony is held or not.[1]

In direct contrast with Tsarist practice, marriage and divorce in the Soviet Union are voluntary acts of the two parties. A distinctive feature of Soviet marriage laws is that in divorce there is no intrusion into the private lives of husband or wife. Yet, though it bases married life on principles of equality and freewill, the Soviet nevertheless wages determined war against a frivolous attitude towards marriage. It considers short-lived liaisons to be distortions of the fundamental aim of marriage—the creation of a healthy family.

Soviet legislation for the protection of women's rights as mothers is of particular importance. The law gives equal rights to, and puts equal responsibility on, both parents where the rearing and education of children are concerned. If a father deserts his family, the State forces him to contribute towards the upkeep of the children until they come of age; and the same obligation is imposed whether the children have been born outside registered marriage or not. A judge gives the amount of these payments in proportion to

[1] " Marriages performed according to religious rites before December 20, 1917, and in districts occupied by the enemy before the establishment of organ so {civil registration, are equivalent to registered marriages."

AND FOR PROTECTION

the father's wages. Under present law, up to 50 per cent of a man's earnings may be requisitioned for the payment of alimony in respect of children. For a man to put the entire burden of rearing children on the mother, or to leave her dependent on State aid only—practices not yet wholly undermined in the U.S.S.R.—are considered criminal offences by the Soviet State and are being mercilessly combated. Non-payment of alimony in respect of children is severely punished. All complaints against defaulting parents are immediately dealt with, and judgments on them put into action forthwith.

Public censure of men who desert children or pregnant wives affords much help in protecting the mother. Public opinion and, above all, the Press, wage a systematic campaign on offenders against the laws of public morality by surrounding them with an atmosphere of general disapprobation. Of great practical significance for women, also, is the law which decrees that if either the former husband or wife is unfit for work after the dissolution of a marriage, the sick party has the right to receive aid from the healthy.

Together with the complete equality of the sexes in personal civil rights, there exists in the Soviet Union complete equality for men and women in all political respects. According to the Soviet Constitution, the right to elect and be elected to the soviets, the supreme organs of authority, is open to all persons of both sexes above eighteen years of age.

But the equality of men and women in political and civil rights is insufficient of itself. Women must also be given the opportunity of making full use of their rights, of giving them practical expression in everyday life, of really standing on equal ground with men. Only then will they emerge from an age-long cultural and social inferiority and from material dependence on their husbands. In the Soviet Union, we are solving this problem chiefly by drawing masses of women into industry and other useful public activities.

The entry of Soviet women into industry assures them of genuine equality with men and of real freedom. It is accompanied by the systematic improving of their qualifications; by the mass attraction of women into training-schools and public life on equal terms with men; and by a fundamental re-organisation of the everyday living conditions of the working woman. Women are being relieved of the burden of unproductive housework, which is being supplanted by communal services. Thus the mass entry of women into industry and public life is made possible, and the conditions necessary for their cultural growth and sure position in the economic life of the country are secured.

AND FOR PROTECTION

Enormous attention is paid to the protection of maternity among woman workers in the U.S.S.R.—that is, to the creation of working conditions that will safeguard the health of both the mother and her child. More than fifty different kinds of work that might be specifically harmful to the female organism are prohibited to women. But there is nothing permanent about this prohibition. As the result of widespread industrial reconstruction, of the increasing mechanisation of labour, and of the vast improvements that are being made in industrial hygiene, the possibility of employing women without injury to their health is continually being extended to new kinds of labour. In addition, specific dangers to the health of women workers in certain kinds of work are being systematically eliminated by appropriate measures.

At the instigation of the Government, a number of important scientific organisations with well-known scientists at their head are engaged on this problem of the employment of women in various kinds of work and the necessary conditions that should accompany it. Some results of this research were used in 1931 and the years following in allocating to different activities the enormous mass of women that had come on the labour market. Soviet law does not allow the employment of women in work that requires great physical effort. Scientific research has shown that women cannot carry a load of more than twenty kilos without injury to their health, and in 1931 a law was passed prohibiting them from doing so.

A comprehensive system of measures is directed towards the general improvement of working conditions, and special inspectors see that these measures are carried out. Every design for the construction of a new factory has to satisfy certain sanitary and technical conditions before it is passed. All this greatly influences the improvement of general sanitary and hygienic conditions in new factories—and in particular those conditions affecting women—and the increased employment of female labour is thus facilitated.

Soviet labour laws on working hours and social insurance are of great importance to the health of workers in general, and of women workers in particular. The seven-hour working day has been fixed by law for the majority of industries: in many other kinds of work (office, professional work, industries with difficult conditions of labour) an even shorter working day—six hours—is the rule. All workers are entitled to a minimum annual holiday of two weeks; and many categories of workers have also the right to supplementary leave, varying in length according to the nature of their employment. These measures regulating hours of work are of much benefit in preserving the health of the workers

AND FOR PROTECTION

and providing them with normal periods for rest and recuperation.

Of enormous significance, both in principle and practice, is the fact that women are paid the same rates as men: "equal pay for equal work."

The Soviet system of social insurance provides all·workers, including women workers, with help whenever, through illness or accident, they are invalided either temporarily or for life. The distinguishing features of this insurance are: that it is extended to all hired workers whether in town or country; and that the funds are supplied by contributions from the business concerns and institutions employing the workers (the workers themselves pay no insurance). According to Soviet law, payments from the insurance funds are made to temporary invalids (illness, accident, quarantine, care of sick members of the family, pregnancy, child-bearing); to chronic invalids (life pension) and old people. Other supplementary payments include those for the death of a breadwinner, for the burial of a member of the family, towards the feeding of a child. In addition, social insurance organisations provide free medical treatment for all insured workers and their families; there are also widespread sanatorium and spa services for workers needing special sanatorium treatment, and a vast net of rest homes for those suffering chiefly from exhaustion and anæmia.

Some idea of the range of this health work may be obtained from the fact that the budget for social insurance in 1935 was 67,000,000 roubles, which was spent on various forms of benefit for insured workers and their families. In 1934, 340,800 workers and members of workers' families visited sanatoriums and rest homes at the expense of the social insurance funds.

Up to 1930, social insurance also paid unemployment benefits; but, with the complete cessation of unemployment, these payments have been nullified.

A system of social insurance with so many ramifications and so enormous a range results in a sharp rise in the standard of living and cultural level of the workers. It gives them security for the morrow, even in the event of unforeseen mishaps, and makes for healthy conditions of work and life. Under such conditions the workers—among them masses of women—who are pouring into all kinds of national activities, become firmly established in their respective careers.

Soviet laws for the protection of motherhood and childhood and for the social insurance of maternity have enormous significance both in principle and practice. The experience of many countries, including pre-revolutionary Russia, shows that without adequate laws for the protection of women workers, the employment of mothers in industry, particularly in factories, leads to widespread organic disease, to difficult and abnormal pregnancies (an increased percentage of miscarriages, premature births, illnesses after birth), and to infant disease and mortality. Soviet legislation strives to protect the working woman and her child from these evils by ensuring that the work of women in industry shall proceed in harmony with their functions as mothers.

Thus Soviet law provides that the woman worker shall take sixteen weeks' obligatory leave for pregnancy and child-bearing. This law applies to all women who receive wages in industry, in agriculture, in transport, in business offices, in co-operative organisations, in domestic work, etc. Some office workers and professional women are entitled to a longer leave than that granted to those engaged in physical work, and the list of such favoured occupations grows year by year as women master new kinds of work. At present, the extra leave is granted to women working as engineering, technical, or agricultural specialists; to women doctors, dressers, and nurses; to those working in the teaching professions and in the arts; to saleswomen, packers, typists, stenographers, and so on.

LAWS ON RIGHTS

In 1935 obligatory leave for pregnancy and child-bearing was extended to all women working in collective farms. Model regulations for the collective farm that were accepted by the second All-Union Conference of Collective Farm Shock-Workers, and approved by the Government, included a measure for the relief of pregnant women and nursing mothers in the collective farms by freeing them for one month before child-bearing and one month after. During these two months the mothers receive half their average earnings.

Soviet law provides for the most important factor in the normal development of a healthy child—breast-feeding. According to the Code of Labour Laws, mothers with children at the breast must, in addition to the ordinary dinner interval, be allowed supplementary intervals for feeding their children (at least once every three and a half hours, with each interval lasting not less than half an hour). These intervals are reckoned as working time. The Soviet Government has also introduced a series of other important measures for the protection of motherhood and childhood. The law for the protection of maternity provides for the transference of pregnant women to less tiring work; it prohibits the dismissal of pregnant women (exceptions are allowed only with the consent of the labour inspector); it prohibits the

AND FOR PROTECTION

sending of pregnant women on missions without their own consent; it prohibits night-work for pregnant women and nursing mothers. All these laws are enforced by the labour inspectors, by committees for the protection of labour in the industrial enterprises themselves, and by a system of legal control.

Obligatory payment of wages during pregnancy and child-bearing is one of the most important, if not the deciding, factor in the protection of motherhood. Leave without payment, or with only a small payment, does not in any way relieve the working mother. During pregnancy and after child-bearing, the worker needs a greater degree of comfort than at other times. Leave without payment would simply make her position more difficult by forcing her to seek temporary casual work, frequently more burdensome than her own, in order to obtain the necessary means of subsistence. In the Soviet Union, social insurance assures, during leave for pregnancy and child-bearing, full pay to those women workers of the ordinary grades who have held the same posts for a year or more; slightly less to those of less than a year's service. In addition, all insured persons and their wives who are in receipt of a wage not exceeding 300 roubles have the right to an additional grant on the birth of a child and to a nursing allowance, which is paid for nine months after the date of birth. The mother and child are also given free medical aid and advice in consultation-clinics, lying-in hospitals, and children's clinics. If there is no room for a sick child in the hospital, the mother is given leave from work by the doctor in charge and receives sick-leave payment for the duration of the child's illness.

Nor is the Soviet State's care of mother and child limited merely to the enforcement of the laws I have mentioned. The State has also created a whole system of institutions for infant welfare and the social education of young children, including crèches, kindergartens, playgrounds, etc., which cover the life of a growing child until it reaches school age.

Moreover, in June 1936 the Government issued a new law for the protection of maternity in which the fundamental principles of Soviet law concerning the rights of women and family and marriage questions are developed much further. This law makes provision for a considerable increase in State aid for mothers. Grants for bearing and nursing children are to be increased. All women engaged in office and intellectual work are to receive the same leave for pregnancy and child-bearing as women engaged in physical labour—that is, four months. There will be extensive State grants for large families: the net of

AND FOR PROTECTION

lying-in hospitals, crèches, and kindergartens will be considerably extended, both in town and country: fathers deserting their families will be liable to an increased sentence of two years' imprisonment for non-payment of alimony in respect of children.

All these measures directed towards safeguarding mothers and children and creating a strong healthy family are closely connected with the legal prohibition of abortions. The law of 1920 permitted abortions, but this measure arose from exceptional circumstances and was of a temporary nature. For years the country had suffered the agonies of war. Economic difficulties made the provision of healthy conditions for the mother impossible and forced a number of women to resort to abortions, notwithstanding the harmful consequences and dangers of this operation. At the present time, the level of material prosperity in the Soviet Union has risen enormously; special care is taken of mothers by the State and all public institutions: and exceptionally favourable conditions have been created for them, which are being further improved by the new law. The Soviet woman can, therefore, fulfil, without any fear of the future, " her obligations as a citizen and mother, responsible for the birth and early education of her children "; and the new law prohibits abortions in the interests of

LAWS ON RIGHTS

women's health and of the further strengthening of healthy family and conjugal relations.

In publishing the new law, the Soviet Government acceded to numerous requests from working women; and, in view of the extreme importance of the project and its significance for vast masses of the population, it put it forward for widespread national discussion before it was passed by the legislative body. The discussion was carried on throughout May and June in newspapers, at meetings, etc., all over the country, and it showed that the vast body of women workers approved of the project. Nevertheless, a number of minor amendments and additions were suggested in the process of discussion, and the majority of them were taken into account in the final drafting of the law.

Such are the principles of Soviet legislation on the rights of women and the protection of women workers—complete civil and political equality for women; an all-round strengthening of the family and the position of women within it; unrestricted entry to all occupations and professions which are not injurious to woman's health; free access to all forms of education; the creation of conditions that facilitate the mass entry of women into industry; and, simultaneously, a vigilant protection of woman's health, her maternal functions, her children. Only in this fashion can an enduring

AND FOR PROTECTION

foundation be laid for the accomplishment of the chief task of the Soviet State in the province of women's work—the securing of complete factual equality between the sexes, and the real emancipation of women.

CHAPTER II

GENERAL RESULTS OF THE DEVELOPMENT OF WOMEN'S WORK IN THE SOVIET UNION

FEMALE LABOUR was fairly widely employed even in Tsarist Russia—largely because its cheapness made it suitable for capitalist exploitation. In 1914 the average daily earnings of a woman worker in industry were 47·7 per cent of those of a man. Women doing the same work as men were paid at a much lower rate. Thus, for example, the average wage of a woman printer in Moscow in 1907 was 13 roubles 90 kopecks a month—40 per cent of a man's wages: and a similar ratio between the earnings of men and women existed in all branches of industry.

From 1900 to 1913, the number of women in Russian manufacturing industries increased from 259,000 to 557,400, and their proportion in the total number of workers from 26·1 per cent to 31·4 per cent. In 1913 there were 636,000 working women in all industries taken together: 24·5

RESULTS OF DEVELOPMENT

per cent of the total number of workers.[1] But they were distributed most unequally among the various industries. Women were chiefly employed in the textile factories—the lowest-paid branch of industry, with the longest working hours.

In 1900, 80 per cent of all women employed in industry were textile workers: in 1913, 67 per cent. Most of them were engaged in unskilled or semi-skilled work, which was in the majority of cases harmful to, or intolerably difficult for, women.

During the Imperialist war the absolute and relative number of working women increased considerably in consequence of the mass mobilisation of men and the growth of war industries. According to approximate figures, 880,000 women were engaged in industry in 1917—31 per cent of the total number of workers.

The general position of working women during the war greatly deteriorated. A longer working day, a decrease in real wages consequent on rising prices, food shortage, mass destruction of bread-winners and relatives at the front—all these calamities fell with particular severity on the working women.

One must add that the cultural level of the woman proletariat was extremely low. It is

[1] These statistics, as well as the following ones relating to the pre-revolutionary period, are taken from the reports of factory and mining inspectors.

enough to point out that in 1918 more than half (56 per cent) of all women members of industrial trade unions were quite illiterate. In other unions and among non-union workers the percentage of illiterates was even higher.

The victory of the Revolution in 1917 laid the foundation of the Soviet State, and caused as fundamental and decisive an upheaval in the sphere of female labour as in all other spheres of social life. The organisation of public services, crèches, kindergartens, communal restaurants and laundries, was begun during the very first years of Soviet rule. They were designed to lighten the burden of domestic toil and free women for socially useful work; in which direction alone could women achieve complete equality with men.

But the conquest of a gloomy and oppressive heritage bequeathed to women by the past—the task of overcoming the effects of centuries of cultural backwardness and tyranny and of raising the level of skill among women workers—was fraught with serious difficulties which could only be vanquished by a complete reorganisation of conditions of life and work throughout the country. In accomplishing this task, the country has lived through a series of stages corresponding to the chief stages of the general economic development of the U.S.S.R.

OF WOMEN'S WORK

During the years of military Communism—1918–21—there was a sharp decline in the number of industrial workers, including women. This was the period when everything was sacrificed to the Civil War. The flower of the proletariat was to be found in the ranks of the Red Army at the front. Many industrial concerns were closed for lack of raw material and fuel; and the most important industrial districts were in the hands of the counter-revolutionaries.

The New Economic Policy in 1921 was responsible for a general revival in the economic life of the country; the number of workers in industry and other branches of national activity began to grow. Year after year witnessed a steady increase in the ranks of women workers. As early as 1926 the number of women engaged in industry exceeded the pre-war level, reaching a figure of 658,500. In 1928, the year preceding the First Five-Year Plan, the figure was 769,300. But up to 1929 the rate of this movement of women into industry only slightly exceeded the rate of the general growth of the proletariat. Consequently, the proportion of women workers remained almost stable—28·1 per cent in 1923, 28·2 per cent in 1926, 28·6 per cent in 1928. An absolute increase in the number of women engaged in all branches of industry can be observed; but it is not always accompanied by an increase in the

RESULTS OF DEVELOPMENT

proportion of women, which latter is to be found chiefly in branches of light industry—for example, the proportion of women in the textile industry grew from 58·7 per cent in 1923 to 61·2 per cent in 1926.

In non-industrial categories, the development of female labour during the reconstruction period is characterised by much the same features as in industry: that is, a growth in the absolute number of women employed, accompanied in some cases by an increase in the proportion of women among the total number of workers (in medical and public health organisations, for instance, the proportion of women increased from 60·7 per cent in 1923 to 65·4 per cent in 1928).

By the first years of the N.E.P., the proportion of women engaged in practically every department of industry and national affairs had already exceeded corresponding pre-war figures. Thus, in industry as a whole, the proportion of women during the years 1923–28 fluctuated between 28 per cent and 29 per cent as compared with 24·5 per cent in 1913. In individual branches of industry very much the same state of affairs existed, as the following figures show[1]:

---

[1] 1913—taken from data collected by factory inspectors.
1926—taken from data of the Central Statistical Administration of the U.S.S.R.

THE NUMBER OF WOMEN WORKERS EXPRESSED IN PERCENTAGES OF THE TOTAL NUMBER OF WORKERS OF BOTH SEXES

	1913 per cent	1926 per cent
All Mining	4·0	7·3
Coal-mining only	3·6	8·3
Metal	4·2	9·2
Wood-working	9·9	15·2
Chemical	39·9	33·5
Food	22·0	26·0
Leather and bootmaking	17·3	18·3
Textile	55·7	59·6
Paper and allied trades	24·0	24·9

Figures that would allow us to trace the history of women in non-industrial occupations during the period under examination, and make a similar comparison with pre-war conditions, are not available for the whole of the U.S.S.R. However, an examination of the figures for Moscow relating to 1912 and 1926 shows the same important absolute and relative growth of female labour in all chief non-industrial occupations. Thus, in Moscow, women constituted 1·5 per cent of the total number of railway and transport workers in 1912, and 8·6 per cent in 1926; among medical and nursing personnel, 56·5 per cent in 1912 and 72 per cent in 1926; among accountants and office staffs, 19·5 per cent in 1912 and 42 per cent in 1926; as saleswomen, 7·1 per cent in 1912 and 15·8 per cent in 1926.¹

Thus we see that in 1926, at the end of the period of recovery, employment of female labour in important occupations was more widespread than before the war. In order, however, fully to appreciate the significance of these figures, we must realise that they also represent quite different qualitative phenomena. In pre-war Russia, female labour was widely employed in factories as the cheapest kind of labour—that which yielded most profit to the factory-owner. To-day the drawing of women into Soviet industry is subordinated to their enfranchisement and the encouragement of their social and cultural development. From the very beginning, women were paid the same wages as men. The employment of female labour in Soviet enterprises does not make for any saving in expenditure; on the contrary, it entails much extra outlay. Besides payments in respect of maternity leave, nursing intervals, etc., considerable sums had to be expended in the construction of various service units. A net of communal services was created literally out of nothing—crèches, kindergartens, communal restaurants serving hundreds of thousands of people. In 1928 the number of children in crèches

¹ *The Annual Statistical Register for Moscow and the Moscow District*, No. 2, published in Moscow 1927, pp. 46–51, 68–74.

was 257,000; in kindergartens, 450,000. In the same year communal restaurants provided 750,000 dinners each day.

During the same period women began to be drawn into various forms of professional and technical training, chiefly into the factory schools. These institutions for making skilled workers out of adolescents were the offspring of the October Revolution, and from the very beginning of their existence, much attention was paid to the problem of attracting girls into them. According to the figures of the State Planning Commission, the number of pupils in factory schools of all types gradually increased from 2,000 in 1921 to 178,300 in 1928. In 1921 the percentage of girl pupils in these schools was 13·3 per cent; by 1928 it had risen to 27·6 per cent.

The attraction of women into industry was accompanied by systematic efforts to raise their cultural level. As we have already stated, rather more than half the women members of industrial trade unions in 1918 were illiterate, whereas the percentage of illiterates among members of both sexes was only 36. By the first year of the First Five-Year Plan the overwhelming majority of women members of trade unions were already literate, and the percentage of illiterates among women in the industrial trade unions was now 15·8 per cent, a figure much nearer the general level of literacy among members of both sexes. (The percentage of illiterates among members of both sexes in the trade unions in 1929 was 7·4.)

The years of the First Five-Year Plan (1929–32) —years of widely developed socialist construction throughout our national life—witnessed decisive changes in the province of female labour. From 1930 onwards, the rate of drawing women into industry in all spheres of socialist production was sharply intensified, and women became firmly entrenched in a whole series of new occupations. During this period the tempestuous growth in our national activities created an urgent demand for more workers, and this ensured favourable conditions for the employment of enormous numbers of women in useful public work.

The Second Five-Year-Plan is a plan for the complete absorption of the enormous socialist accumulation of the First Five-Year Plan—a plan for further gigantic growth in all branches of socialist production, based on a far-reaching technical reconstruction, and for a rapid increase in the material and cultural well-being of workers in both town and country. The entry of women into industry and public life is a necessary condition for the accomplishment of these aims.

Therefore problems of female labour, even in the Second Five-Year Plan, remain among the most important and decisive factors in socialist construction as a whole.

During the operation of the First and Second Five-Year Plans all the necessary conditions have been created for the widest possible absorption of women into public work. This period is marked by a rapid improvement in all those kinds of communal services that set women free for industry and which will be described in detail in one of the following chapters.

One of the most serious obstacles to the employment of women in a number of trades is the fact that the work entails physical effort beyond their strength; and the most important feature of the technical reorganisation of all branches of industry during the First and Second Five-Year Plan periods has been the mechanisation of these physically burdensome processes. By the end of the Second Five-Year Plan, 80 per cent of the fundamental processes of building are to be mechanised; and almost complete mechanisation will have taken place in coal-mining, coal-hewing, and allied processes. Extremely widespread mechanisation is also being carried out in machine construction, metallurgy, the food and timber industries, numerous branches of light industry, and so on. Moreover, the technical progress which is transforming the whole industrial face of the Soviet Union is characterised by a growing subdivision of labour—the supplanting of handicraft and semi-handicraft trades, which demand long apprenticeship, by mass processes which are much more easily learnt by workers who have received a general cultural and technical training. This also considerably simplifies the problem of drawing women into industry.

These new channels for the employment of female labour have been widely exploited both in industry and in other branches of national life. The total number of women workers and employees increased from 3,304,000 in 1929 (the first year of the First Five-Year Plan) to 6,007,000 in 1932 (the last year of the First Five-Year Plan), and to 7,881,000 in 1935. Thus the number of women workers and employees has increased by 4,500,000 during the last six years.

More than a third—about 1,700,000—of these recruits to the ranks of women workers are in large-scale industry; of the rest 400,000 in building; 700,000 in commerce and communal food services; 750,000 in educational and health institutions; and 250,000 in administrative and public institutions.

In all branches of national activity, with the exception of agriculture, with which I shall deal later, the ranks of women workers have grown more rapidly than those of the men. Thus the proportion of women in practically all spheres of labour shows a considerable increase. This is clear from the table on p. 38.

This table also shows that the proportion of women grew at unequal rates in different branches of national economy. During the period of the First and Second Five-Year Plans there is no marked growth in those branches where, earlier, female labour had predominated. Thus, among educational workers, the proportion of women increased from 53 per cent in 1929 to 56·6 per cent in 1935; among workers in health services, from 64·6 per cent to 71·2 per cent.

A more noticeable growth may be observed in branches chiefly employing male labour. Especially characteristic of the First and Second Five-Year Plans is woman's conquest of a whole series of industries and professions quite new to her. Thus, in the building trades, the proportion of women increased from 7 per cent in 1929 to 19·7 per cent in 1935— almost threefold; in transport, the proportion of women was doubled, from 8 to 16·6 per cent; in administrative institutions it grew by half from 19 to 30·8 per cent; in commerce from 15·5 to 30·8 per cent; and in communal restaurants from 46·4 to 63 per cent.

At the same time there is a sharp decrease in the number of women employed in daily work

RESULTS OF DEVELOPMENT

THE NUMBER AND PROPORTION OF WOMEN WORKERS AND EMPLOYEES IN DIFFERENT DEPARTMENTS OF LABOUR

	1929		1933		1935	
	In thousands	In per cent to total member of workers	In thousands	In per cent	In thousands	In per cent
In national economy as a whole ..	3,304	27·2	6,908	30·5	7,881	33·4
Large-scale industry	939	27·9	2,207	34·5	2,627	38·3
Building trades	64	7·0	437	16·0	450	19·7
Transport	104	8·0	322	13·8	384	16·6
Commerce and public food services	134	19·0	786	40·5	822	39·4
Educational, health and administrative institutions	961	38·2	1,766	45·2	1,978	48·8
Agriculture	441	28·0	508	24·2	685	27·0

and domestic service. In 1929 this group comprised a sixth part (16 per cent) of the general body of working women; by 1935 it had decreased to 2·4 per cent. On the other hand, the number of women employed in industry, transport, and building during this period increased from 33 per cent to 44 per cent. This redistribution of female labour among more productive kinds of work is altogether characteristic of the reconstruction period in the Soviet Union.

The most considerable achievements of women workers have been in industry: and the following table shows the growth in the number of women employed in large-scale industries during the periods of the First and Second Five-Year Plans:

	January 1 1929	1933	July 1 1935
Total number of women workers in thousands	804·0	1,826·2	2,321·9
Proportion of women in percentage of the whole	28·8	35·5	39·5

In the middle of 1935 the number of women in industry was 3·6 times the pre-war number, and 5·7 times the number for 1923. Particularly interesting are statistics of the distribution of this colossal army of working women created under the First Five-Year Plan.

In the Soviet Union, as we have already noted,

RESULTS OF DEVELOPMENT

the development of heavy industry under the First Five-Year Plan was particularly intensive; and its chief branches (metal, mining, chemical) were therefore in urgent need of new workers. This accelerated the absorption of vast numbers of women into these branches of industry. In addition, it was just these industries which were being fundamentally reorganised by mechanisation and the introduction of other measures. As we have already emphasised, these developments increase the possibility of employing female labour without injury to women's health and maternal functions. Particularly characteristic, therefore, of the First Five-Year Plan is the increased absorption of women into heavy industry, in which they had earlier been employed only to a negligible degree. (On January 1, 1929, women constituted only 11·3 per cent of the total number of workers in heavy industry, whereas in light industry they constituted 50 per cent.)

More than half the influx of women into industry during the years of the First and Second Five-Year Plans was directed into heavy industry. In the metal industries, the number of women employed grew from 50,000 in 1929 to 434,000 in 1935. Consequently, there was a parallel increase in the proportion of women in heavy industry.

Here are the changes in the proportion of

women in individual branches of industry during the First Five-Year Plan period:

PROPORTION OF WOMEN IN PERCENTAGE OF THE WHOLE

	1929 (average figures)	Jan. 1, 1933	July 1, 1935
Industry as a whole	28·3	35·5	39·5
Coal-mining	8·0	17·5	24·0
Metal	9·2	21·9	25·8
Chemical	34·4	39·3	40·0
Wood-working	19·1	32·0	39·7
Paper and allied trades	25·8	34·3	41·4
Leather and Fur	23·3	44·4	56·2
Cotton	62·3	68·5	69·8
Sewing	—	81·4	82·6
Food	26·6	34·4	44·9

This table shows the growth (proportionately) of female labour in all branches of industry, both heavy and light; it also shows that in heavy industry this growth was very much more rapid than in light.

During the operation of the Second Five-Year Plan, and side by side with the further growth of heavy industry and the intensive development of light industry and the food industries, there took place a notable increase in the absolute and relative number of women workers in many branches of these industrial groups (leather, paper, food); and in consequence there was a radical change in the distribution of women workers throughout

RESULTS OF DEVELOPMENT

the different branches during the First and Second Five-Year Plans. In Tsarist Russia, at the beginning of the twentieth century, four-fifths of all women engaged in industry were employed in the textile factories. At the outset of the World War, the proportion was two-thirds, and in 1929 the preponderance of textile workers among women in industry still persisted.

But with the implementing of the First Five-Year Plan the position changes sharply. The textile worker ceases to be the most familiar figure among working women. On January 1, 1933, only 39 per cent of the total number of working women is to be found in the textile industry, and on July 1, 1935, only 31·7 per cent. On the other hand, the proportion of women in heavy industry shows a marked increase. In 1929 less than a quarter of all women industrial workers were engaged in heavy industry (22·4 per cent); by June 1933 the proportion had risen to more than half (50·2 per cent). Before the war, only 2·4 per cent of all women industrial workers were employed in the metal industry; in 1935, 18·7 per cent. Women engaged in the metal industries, as skilled electricians, in various chemical industries—these are the main figures in the army of women industrial workers created by the First Five-Year Plan.

OF WOMEN'S WORK

These changes have had an enormous significance in the development of the Soviet woman worker—as is shown not only by the fact that women have entrenched themselves in a wide range of industries where formerly they were hardly ever found, but, above all, that they have mastered the most highly skilled work—work which to the greatest degree guarantees the development of their powers as producers.[1] This leads to an increased degree of material prosperity among women, since these new kinds of work invariably carry with them higher wages.

These successes are all the more praiseworthy since they were accompanied by a further improvement in the health of women workers. There is a fairly widespread theory that women cannot be employed in heavy industry to any real extent because much of the work is either too exhausting for them or in some way or other specifically harmful. I have devoted a special chapter to this subject—Chapter VI, " Towards a Healthier Life for Women." Here I shall merely note that Soviet practice has completely belied such theories. The policy of the Soviet authorities directed towards making women's work easier and healthier, and a general raising of the material and cultural standard of life among men and women workers, has produced

[1] For details see Chapter III.

RESULTS OF DEVELOPMENT

an enormous increase in the number of women workers without any increase in the amount of illness among women. On the contrary, the illness rate has declined. Thus the amount of illness among women employed in machine-construction decreased by 25 per cent during the years 1930-34; in the cotton industry by 20 per cent, and so on.

Women are now more prevalent in co-operative industry. At the beginning of 1928 the number of women in co-operatives was 265,000; by the end of the First Five-Year Plan (January 1, 1933) co-operative industry had already absorbed 702,600 women, the majority (70 per cent) of whom were to be found in the textile, sewing, and knitting co-operatives—all handicraft industries traditional to women.

The proportion of women in the general body of co-operative workers during this period increased from 26·4 per cent to 43·5 per cent. During the period of the Second Five-Year Plan the number of women in consumers' co-operatives continued to grow, and this movement was particularly encouraged by the mechanisation of a number of handicraft trades, which made the work considerably easier for women.

Let us now turn to agriculture, which from 1930 onwards was completely reorganised on socialist principles — a reorganisation which exerted an enormous influence on the social and economic position of women in the villages and on the development of agricultural work for women.[1]

From a policy of limiting the exploiting tendencies of the kulaks, the Soviet authorities proceeded to the liquidation of the kulak class by means of wholesale collectivisation. Soviet farms, large State agricultural enterprises, began to be widely organised. These farms attracted large numbers of agricultural workers. Machine and tractor stations were created in collectivised districts, and the village boys and girls were taught how to drive tractors, combines, and other complicated agricultural machines. Former peasants are becoming qualified workers without, however, severing their ties with the village.

The bulk of peasant holdings have been organised into collective farms. By the beginning of 1936, 87·8 per cent of all peasant holdings and 93·9 of land under cultivation were incorporated in these farms, whereas in 1928 the percentage of collectivised peasant holdings was 1·7 per cent and the land belonging to them 1·2 per cent of the total acreage. In the course of this transition the bulk of the women peasants became members of the collective farms.

[1] For details see Chapter IV, " Women in Collectivisation."

RESULTS OF DEVELOPMENT

At first the women peasants did not always display full consciousness of the problems involved in collectivisation. This was reflected in a low standard of discipline, in frequent absence from work, in a fall in productivity. But between 1933 and 1935 the mass of women peasants changed their attitude. Discipline was established, the spirit of co-operation among the women, and the productivity of their labour rose sharply. About 85 per cent of the women members of the collective farms took part in the agricultural campaigns of 1933. Women began to participate extensively in administrative work: they became a powerful force in the collective farms. For millions of women peasants, for the first time in history, the collective farms opened the way to cultural and social development, to complete equality with men, to a cultured and well-to-do existence. This is the chief achievement of collectivisation in the sphere of women's work. It also represents one of the outstanding successes of collectivisation as a whole.

The growth in the number of workers engaged in all branches of our industrial and national activities and, in particular, the increase in the number of women at work, were accompanied by extremely important changes in the general structure of society. Until 1929-30 there remained as a heritage from the past a certain amount of unemployment, which was fed by the steady migration of a large part of the rural population to the towns. Peasants formerly fled to the towns because a small peasant holding with its meagre yield could not feed an entire family. The mass collectivisation of peasant holdings that has taken place since 1930 has fundamentally altered this state of affairs. The transition from individual to collective cultivation of the land, by improving the condition of the poor and middle-class peasants, has destroyed the chief cause of unemployment. The headlong movement from the villages of those in search of work was definitely curtailed. On the other hand, the demand for workers increased. Even in 1929, when the number of unemployed was comparatively high (on May 1 there were 1,772,000 unemployed in the Soviet Union, 49 per cent of whom were women), the demand for labour had already begun to exceed the supply (to the extent of about 28 per cent). In 1930 there were already 160 vacancies for every 100 applications. Consequently the unemployed were quickly absorbed, and by the middle of 1930 unemployment was finally liquidated. Simultaneously, of course, unemployment completely ceased among women, and the most terrible concomitant of unemployment—prostitution—was done away with.

RESULTS OF DEVELOPMENT

The social and economic changes in the Soviet Union resulting from the successful achievements of the First Five-Year Plan, three years of the Second Five-Year Plan, and the general policy of the State, were reflected in the well-being of the country and its inhabitants. The possibility of a recrudescence of unemployment was completely destroyed. This gave all workers, including women, complete confidence in the future and the freedom to choose their profession.

What are the fundamental factors of the success that has been achieved in drawing women into industry?

The assimilation of women into all branches of national activity proceeded during the First Five-Year Plan (and is proceeding at the present time) not in a haphazard, unorganised fashion, but according to definite plans for recruiting reserves of workers. General plans for national production control the operative details—in particular, the plans for introducing female labour into industry that have been now established for different branches of production, for different districts and republics, and for the Soviet Union as a whole.

What is particularly important is that the general scheme of the Soviet Government in drawing women into industry has met with a vast immediate response from women workers of the town and country. This chiefly is responsible for the enormous successes in this sphere.

One of the most important achievements of the First Five-Year Plan was an all-round increase in the material and cultural well-being of the mass of workers. The average annual wage of the proletariat during the First Five-Year Plan was more than doubled (203 per cent); and during the three years of the Second Five-Year Plan it increased by half as much again (159 per cent). Together with the increase in individual earnings, State expenditure on the cultural and everyday needs of the workers is growing rapidly. In 1929 State expenditure on these services for the family of a worker engaged in heavy industry amounted to a monthly average of 28·5 roubles, whereas in 1935 it was 100·2 roubles—almost four times as much.

Another important factor in the growth of well-being among Soviet workers is the increase in the number of wage-earners in a family. In 1929 the average number was 1·2; in 1935, 1·47. This naturally leads to a higher standard of living. The average income of a worker's family in 1935 was 425·3 roubles, as against 132·7 roubles in 1929.

For the mass of women, one of the most important incentives to work was the urge to increase their material and cultural well-being, and the knowledge that by work they could attain this result. At the present time millions of women workers have already achieved a well-to-do and cultured life.

The marked changes in the employment of female labour in various branches of national activity during the First and Second Five-Year Plans have brought about significant changes in the general aspect of the urban female population. In the towns of the Soviet Union on January 1, 1927, only 28·6 per cent of women of working age were earning their own living. By April 1931 the percentage of self-supporting women had increased to 32 per cent. According to approximate estimates, the number of self-supporting women had risen to more than 38 per cent of the urban female population by the end of the First Five-Year Plan.

This growth of independence is to be observed among all women of working age, but it proceeded at different rates of intensity in different age groups. The largest influx into industry and other branches of national production was that of adolescents just beginning to work and of young married women. During the period 1926–31, 33·13 per cent (in different age groups) of the total number of young women between the ages of fifteen and twenty-four were drawn into industry, and 13·5 per cent of the women between the ages of twenty-five and forty-four. In the older groups, the transition to independence was very much less marked, and did not bring about any fundamental changes in the structure of the female population. This resulted in a noticeable lowering of the age-level among women workers. Of the young urban female population (twenty-four years), 32 per cent were self-supporting in 1927 and 40 per cent in 1931. In 1935 there were 803,000 young women workers in large-scale industry, as compared with 200,000 in 1930. In 1935 they constituted 40 per cent of the total number of women engaged in industry.

From what social sources were women recruited to industry at this period? An analysis and comparison of the census of December 1, 1926, and that of April 1, 1931, shows that, in the interval between these two dates, 41 per cent of all additions to the urban female proletariat had come from the villages, and 32·4 per cent were recruits from the dependent urban population (housewives, young people finishing their studies). But by 1931, and particularly in the years following, the marked changes we have described began to make themselves felt. Peasants ceased to migrate from the villages; the urge to work among domestic elements in the towns increased.

Statistics of the All-Union Central Council of Trade Unions for 1931 show that the overwhelming majority—73 per cent, to be exact—of women who entered the trade unions in 1931 were working as hired labour for the first time. It is also particularly essential to note that a considerable percentage of the women who poured into industry in 1931 had formerly lived at home; 13·7 per cent were housewives, and 17 per cent chiefly dependent members of the family. Thus, in the first half of 1931, about 30 per cent of all new female reinforcements in industry came straight from the home. The proportion of such women in the total number of women new to employment is about 43 per cent. A considerable part (26 per cent) of the new ranks of women workers consisted of students entering industry straight from school.

In 1931 we find much the same state of affairs in other non-industrial trade unions and in non-industrial departments of production. In 1932, in the majority of trade unions, there is a further increase in the contribution of urban sources to the new ranks of women workers. According to the estimates of the State Planning Commission, during the First Five-Year Plan, 1,400,000 of the adult urban female population were drawn into industry for the first time. In 1931–32 there is a considerable decrease in the influx of women from the country. In 1931, only 16·9 per cent of new additions to the ranks of women industrial workers came from the villages, whereas, as we have already noted, the influx from the villages in 1927–31 constituted 41 per cent of all new recruits. We already know the reason for this decrease. It was due to an increase in the material prosperity of the rural population produced by the mass collectivisation of peasant holdings.

These statistics serve as a graphic illustration to the words of Stalin: " The village can no longer be called the stepmother of the peasant. And for that very reason the peasant is beginning to settle down in the village, and there is no longer that flight of the muzhik from the village into the town and the automatic influx of labour power."[1] These words are also entirely applicable to women peasants.

The fact that the female proletariat, particularly after 1930, was predominantly recruited from urban sources, resulted in the women workers being more proletarian in origin than the men. Among male workers in 1931 only 30 per cent were children of workers; among women, 43 per cent. This was also due to the active policy of the Soviet authorities in drawing into industry wives and other members of workers' families—a policy primarily directed towards increasing the material well-being of the family as a whole, and

[1] Stalin, *Leninism*, vol. ii, " New Conditions—New Tasks " (speech delivered at the Conference of Leaders of Industry, June 23, 1931), p. 372.

RESULTS OF DEVELOPMENT

thereby creating stable groups of workers closely attached to their factories. Thus the Kolomensk machine-building factory employed, in 1931, over 25 per cent of all women members of workers' families, and 47·8 per cent of the total number of childless workers' wives. In the Ural machine-building factory we have an even higher figure. Here, in 1931, 44 per cent of all women members of workers' families were employed; this number included 43·9 per cent of workers' wives and 66·2 per cent of childless wives. A similar state of affairs existed in other branches of industry.

From the narrow confines of domesticity the Soviet woman took to the high road of public work. Here she has vast scope for the development of her creative talents. The widespread absorption of women into all branches of national work and industry is the first manifestation of the public activity stimulated among women by socialist construction.

In the Soviet Union the absorption of women into public work is linked up with their complete social re-education. The Second Five-Year Plan set itself the task of transforming the entire population of the Union into conscious builders of socialism. We have achieved great things in this direction, particularly among women.

The successes of socialist reconstruction, the extraordinarily rapid development of industry, the increase in the productivity of labour, which characterise the First and Second Five-Year Plans are largely founded on the widespread development of socialist methods of organising labour. Socialist competition is based on the realisation among workers that their personal interests and the general interests of production are identical; on an understanding of that fundamental tenet of the Soviet system that a man's labour is not for others but for himself. Socialist competition and its chief method of organisation, shock-work, are powerful factors in raising the productivity of labour and strengthening its discipline. At the same time, they are an indication of the growth of social and political consciousness among the working class and an expression of its creative initiative. In this mighty advance, woman, whose past was such a serious obstacle to her social and political development, does not fall behind man; she is to be found in the same ranks, marching at his side.

In 1936 the Stakhanovite movement—called by the name of its initiator, a coal-miner of the Don Basin, Alexei Stakhanov—spread throughout the length and breadth of the Soviet Union. This is the supreme manifestation of socialist competition among workers. It is based on the cultural and creative enthusiasm of the workers; it aims at increasing the productivity of labour

RESULTS OF DEVELOPMENT

and far surpassing established norms. In many branches of industry (coal-mining, machine-building, textiles), the productivity of the Stakhanovites has far exceeded the technical norms and record achievements of the leading industrial countries of the world. The range of the movement may be gauged from the fact that three or four months after its inception 25 per cent of the total number of workers in the chief branches of industry were Stakhanovites. In January 1936, of 232,000 workers in 55 machine-building factories, 24 per cent were Stakhanovites. By February 1936, 19·8 per cent of the workers in the cotton industry had entered the Stakhanovite ranks.

In many industries women are in the foremost ranks; and many outstanding heroes of labour have emerged from their midst. The Soviet Government has decorated 89 women workers with the Order of Lenin, the Order of the Red Banner of Labour, and the Sign of Honour Order for splendid achievements in their work and brilliant successes in mastering technique. They include the weavers E. and M. Vinogradova, T. Odintzova, E. Fadeeva, the knitting-machine operator E. Fedorova, and many other women leaders of industry who are famous throughout the country as eminent examples of the development of working women in the Soviet Union.

OF WOMEN'S WORK

No less significant are the successes achieved by Soviet women in agriculture. The rapid growth, year by year, of the cultural and productive standards of workers on collective and state farms resulted in 1935 in achievements in output unrivalled throughout the world. In the agricultural campaign of 1935 the so-called " campaign of the five-hundreders " among the collective farm workers in the beet-fields was organised on the initiative of Maria Demchenko. It aimed at gathering a harvest of 500 centners (centner=100 lbs.) from every hectare of land, the average norm throughout the Union in 1935 being 132 centners. This campaign was crowned with amazing success.

Quite extraordinary standards of productivity were established in the campaign by women leaders in the collective and Soviet cotton farms of Uzbekistan, Tadjikistan, Turkmenistan, and Kazakstan. Before the Revolution the women of these eastern people were veritable slaves, living in the complete seclusion of their husbands' house. Now many of them have emerged into public work and public life. They have fully mastered the technique of cotton-growing, and in 1935 they achieved a record cotton harvest. The names of such women are surrounded with an aura of fame throughout the Union. In 1935, also, many outstanding workers came to the fore in the ranks of women cattle-breeders. On March 1, 1936, 724 women from various branches of agriculture were given the highest awards of the Union for their exceptional achievements in production, and outstanding efficiency in their work (cf. Chapters IV and VII).

Thus the mass attraction of women into production in the Soviet Union is accompanied by their rapid social development and an enormous increase in their productive powers. In the following chapters we shall follow up this development in all its chief manifestations.

It must not be supposed that these successes were easily achieved. On the contrary, the Soviet authorities were obliged to fight against the low opinion of women as workers that was held by many conservative elements, in the trade unions and elsewhere and among the backward elements of the peasantry. This antagonism was particularly evident in the collective farms. At the present time these prejudices have generally been overcome. Stalin's dictum that "woman is a powerful force in the collective farms" has become in practice one of the fundamental principles of collectivised agriculture. As in agriculture, so in other branches of national activity—the drive for a widespread and vigorous assimilation of women has become general.

CHAPTER III

WOMAN AS A SKILLED WORKER

THE SORT OF WORK a woman does and the training required for this work are the deciding factors where her absorption into industry is concerned. Skilled work gives her a specialised training and the opportunity of improving her qualifications, and thus increasing her earnings. It also ensures her the most favourable conditions from the point of view of health. Unskilled labour almost always demands physical effort beyond the powers of the female organism; skilled labour is to a much lesser degree dependent on physical considerations.

The social and political significance that lies in the mastering of skilled trades by women is enormous. The real liberation and equality of women cannot be secured without overcoming the backwardness of women as skilled workers. Only when she is trained can the woman stand on equal ground with the man in industrial, social, and cultural life; because only skilled work will provide her with the conditions of life that are necessary for her cultural growth.

For this reason the Soviet authorities have always considered the general problem of drawing women into socialist industry in conjunction with that of improving the qualifications of the working woman. In Government decrees concerning female labour—particularly in those of the Third Session of the Central Executive Committee—these problems are shown to be inseparable. It is emphasised that, in order to provide our national industrial life with future reserves of workers, special attention must be paid to improving the training of women and to drawing them into industry.

From the pre-war period the Soviet Union inherited a tradition of badly trained female labour. Women were employed almost exclusively in unskilled and semi-skilled work, both in industry and other branches of national life. A long period of time and much systematic work were needed to overcome this backwardness. Even to-day the problem cannot be said to have been entirely solved.

In 1927, the tenth year of the existence of the Soviet Government, the level of skill among women in every branch of industry was considerably lower than that of the men. This is clearly shown by the distribution of men and

SKILLED WORKER

women workers on the tables which regulate wages in the Soviet Union according to the degree of skill employed.[1] In 1927 the five lowest categories covering unskilled and semi-skilled labour included 83 per cent of all women employed in industry and only 41 per cent of the men. The highest categories show 24 per cent of men and 1 per cent of women. Even in the textile industry, traditional occupation of women, the level of skill among women workers in 1927 was very much lower than that of the men. In the unskilled and semi-skilled categories there were 14·7 per cent men and 38·1 per cent women; in highly skilled categories, 24·9 per cent men and 3·8 per cent women.

Practically all the women engaged in heavy industry, particularly in machine building, were employed as unskilled labour.

In 1928–30 (the first half of the First Five-Year Plan) the overwhelming majority of women employed in industry still represented unskilled labour; but there is a noticeable improvement in the training of women directed towards equalising the proportions of male and female labour. Thus in metallurgy during 1928–30 the proportion of unskilled workers to the total

[1] In the Soviet Union, workers are at the present time divided into eight grades of qualification, so that the lower grades include the less skilled workers, the middle grades (4–5) workers of average skill, and the higher grades (6–8) highly skilled workers. In 1927 the number of grades was much higher, and not alike for all industries.

number of women workers decreased from 84 per cent to 74 per cent.

In 1929–30 the proportion of unskilled women employed in the manufacture of agricultural machinery decreased from 91·2 per cent to 83 per cent. This improvement was also apparent in other branches of industry (textiles, bootmaking); but right up to 1930 there was no essential change in the general character of female labour. In 1930, the overwhelming majority of women employed in practically all branches of industry still represented unskilled or semi-skilled labour. Quite a different state of things is to be found at the end of the First Five-Year Plan in 1932. By this time, as a result of colossal efforts in training women for work and in improving the qualifications of others, the position shows a marked change.

In metallurgy and the cotton industry in 1930–32, women were thus distributed according to skill:

Category of skill	Percentage of women workers	
	1930	1932
Ferrous Metal Industry		
Highly-skilled	0·1	0·2
Skilled	1·2	6·5
Semi-skilled	24·6	36·7
Unskilled	74·1	56·6
Cotton Industry		
Highly-skilled	0·9	2·8
Skilled	37·8	49·2
Semi-skilled	38·2	30·3
Unskilled	23·1	17·7

SKILLED WORKER

The same sort of improvement can be observed over the period 1930–32 among women workers employed in machine-building. In 1930, unskilled workers in the different branches of machine construction constituted 72–84 per cent of the total number; in 1932 there were only 40 per cent, the bulk of the remainder (56 per cent) now being employed in semi-skilled work, and only a very small proportion (4 per cent) in skilled or highly skilled work.

The limited participation of women in highly skilled work at the end of the First Five-Year Plan can be easily understood. Work of this kind demands long experience; and the average industrial experiences of women is still, naturally enough, shorter than that of men—it is only during the last six years—1930–35—that there has been a considerable influx of women into industry.

According to trade-union records of 1932–33, the average working experience of a male worker in ferrous metals was 6·9 years, that of a woman 2·9; in motor-car construction, for a man 7·7, for a woman 3·2; in the construction of motor-tractors, the average for a man was 7·4 years, for a woman 2·6; in electrical engineering, for a man 7·4, for a woman 4·1.[1]

Women's ever-increasing participation in skilled

---

[1] Statistical section of the All-Union Council of Trade Unions, Bullet No. 2, 1934, p. 9.

labour is shown by a comparison of the census of occupations for 1927 with that of October 1934. Over this period the participation of women in the construction of industrial machinery shows a marked increase. In agricultural machine-building in 1927 women constituted only 0·8 per cent of the turners, at the end of 1934 the proportion was 23·8 per cent; among milling-cutters the figures were 3·8 per cent in 1927 and 37·8 per cent in 1934; among polishers, 8·1 per cent in 1927, 39·8 per cent in 1934, etc.

A similar rate of growth may be observed among the number of women engaged in various other branches of machine construction and in the electrical industry. In a whole series of mechanical processes women are in the majority. In 1927, women employed in drilling processes in agricultural machine construction numbered 10 per cent, in 1934 there were 73·6 per cent; among turret lathe operators in the electrical industry there were 11 per cent women in 1927 and 59 per cent in 1934. The employment of women as minders for various kinds of machines (hammers, cranes, windlasses) increased just as strikingly—from 1·2 per cent in 1927 to 30–50 per cent in 1934. This widespread introduction of women into mechanical industry is closely bound up with the widespread mechanisation and automatic working of industrial processes which

SKILLED WORKER

formerly demanded great physical strength and long training.

Changes in technical processes and in the organisation of production and labour have made possible the entry of women into a whole series of other mechanical trades. The introduction of conveyor assembling enormously increased the number of women employed in the assembling departments, and the percentage of women employed as assemblers of agricultural machinery grew from 1·6 per cent in 1927 to 25·5 per cent in 1934. To-day women are widely employed in the most highly skilled metallurgical processes. Among machine repairers in the motor-tractor industry, 14 per cent are now women; in 1927 there were no women engaged in this work.

In metallurgical industries the furnace-rooms (blast furnace, open hearth furnace, rolling mill) are closed to women, since they demand considerable physical effort which might prove harmful to the female organism. But women are fairly extensively used in working certain machinery (about 10–40 per cent as minders of various cranes and installations in different trades).

In electric power stations, women were practically never employed as unskilled labour in 1927. In 1934 they formed 13 per cent of the fitters on ordinary duty and 32 per cent of those at the main switchboard.

Women are being widely employed in the skilled departments of the printing industry (compositors, proof-readers); in the paper industry; and in bootmaking. Widespread mechanisation of the sawmills has opened the woodworking industry to women. In the more skilled work of the sawmills (gang-sawing and saw-fitting), women were employed to a negligible extent (0·3 per cent to 1·4 per cent) in 1927; by the end of 1934, the figure had risen to 12 per cent.

In the cotton industry, practically all the skilled work of the spinning-mills was formerly done by women; and by the end of 1934 male labour had almost been crowded out of the weaving-mills. In 1934, 97 per cent of the total number of weavers were women as compared with 87 per cent in 1927. In the dyeing and finishing rooms, the employment of skilled female labour increased to a very large extent. Particular emphasis must be laid on the success of women in mastering the most highly skilled processes of the textile industry. In 1927 there were hardly any women loom-repairers; in 1934 they formed 7 per cent of the total number. The number of women apprentices also increased rapidly.

Women show equally striking achievements in mastering skilled trades in other branches of trade and industry. In the building trades, the growth of women's participation in skilled labour

SKILLED WORKER

was particularly intensive. In the census of December 1, 1926, only 900 women are registered in the building trades, of whom 700 were engaged in skilled work. By April 1, 1931, the number of women had already increased to 17,000—3·6 per cent of the total number of workers. But the greatest achievements of women in these trades belong to subsequent years. The percentage of women plasterers rose from 18 per cent in 1932 to 32 per cent at the end of 1934; of motor-minders from 22 per cent in 1932 to 39 per cent in 1934, etc. The number of women increases in proportion to the increasing mechanisation of building, which is being transformed from a primitive, badly organised industry into one demanding only a limited application of physical effort.

According to the census of 1926 and the town registration of 1931, the number of women doing skilled work on the railways increased sevenfold during the years 1926 to 1931. During the period 1932–35, the percentage of women working on the trains increased from 8·5 per cent to 14·9 per cent; on the lines from 17·4 per cent to 22·4 per cent; and on the telephones and telegraphs from 33 per cent to 35·5 per cent.

The employment of skilled women workers in other kinds of transport grew even more rapidly than on the railways. From 1926 to 1931 (according to the same sources of information) women began to form a majority among tram-conductors—61·1 per cent in 1931 as compared with 39 per cent in 1926. The percentage of women tram-drivers increased from 3·2 per cent in 1926 to 13·3 per cent in 1931; among chauffeurs, from 0·2 per cent to 3·2 per cent. Subsequent years see a further increase of female employment in these occupations.

The training and re-training of women for participation in all the skilled trades began in 1930. We have already noted the achievements of the reconstruction period in this sphere. Let us now look at the results of the First Five-Year Plan and some years of the Second.

The children of workers form one of the most important sources of labour power in the Soviet Union. Young people, after receiving a general education (an obligatory seven-year course), can, at their own wish, enter factory, transport, or agricultural schools, which train them as skilled workers by a combination of theoretical instruction and practical work in school and factory workshops. The number of such schools increased rapidly during the operation of the First Five-Year Plan; and the number of pupils in them grew from 178,300 in 1928 to 958,900 on January 1, 1933.

Girls have joined these schools at a greater rate than boys, with the result that the percentage of girl pupils has considerably increased. Thus the percentage of girls in the industrial factory schools increased from 24·9 in 1929 to 38·4 in 1932. At the beginning of 1929 the number of girls was 41,400; on January 1, 1933, it was 162,800—four times as many. The most striking increase was in the factory schools for heavy industry—in ferrous metals, from 14·3 per cent on January 1, 1930, to 27·5 per cent on January 1, 1933; in machine-building, from 12·7 per cent to 26·8 per cent; in electrical engineering, from 30·6 per cent to 35·1 per cent.

During the period of the Second Five-Year Plan, the number of pupils in the factory schools somewhat diminished as a result of shortening the tuition period, but the proportion of female pupils continued to increase. Thus the percentage of girls in the schools for heavy industry for 1932 rose from 26·5 to 27·7—a rise which includes an increase in the machine-building schools from 26·8 per cent to 29 per cent.

These successes in drawing girls into skilled work are the result of the general policy of the Soviet authorities with regard to female labour —a policy directed towards the many-sided improvement of women's qualifications. Special laws have been passed by the Soviet Government towards this end. Thus in 1931, the year which marked the entry of the largest number of women into industry, it was decreed that 50 per cent of all further pupils in the factory schools (the chief centre for training young people as skilled workers) must be girls. In 1935 this decree was extended to the agricultural schools.

The enormous development of industrial training for women and girls is likewise based on their growing desire to work in industry, particularly in callings new to women. In former years, girls took little interest in improving their qualifications, especially in occupations new to them. In the majority of cases they regarded their work in industry as temporary. As a general rule they entered "masculine" trades most unwillingly, and strove to become dressmakers or cotton workers rather than ironworkers or turners, and frequently left the factory schools for courses in dressmaking or typewriting.

But the last few years have witnessed a striking change in the attitude of women and girls towards the choice of a vocation and vocational training. During these years, the task of improving workers' qualifications and giving them a thorough technical training, particularly in heavy industry, became a deciding factor in socialist construction. Influenced by this, as is shown by researches carried out in 1930–31, there sprang up among women and girls an enormous urge towards industrial training. This was particularly noticeable in the field of metallurgy. " I want to be a turner or a milling cutter," is the answer often met with in questionnaires given to members of workers' families. The actions of girls on finishing training also bears witness to this change of attitude. Whereas in 1926–27 only 66–68 per cent of the girls in the Kolomensk factory stayed on as workers on leaving the factory school, the percentage in 1930–31 was 97.

An examination of the pupils of the factory school of the Moscow " Electrocombinat " at the end of the First Five-Year Plan, showed, in general, equally satisfactory results with the girls as the boys, and, in particular, that the girls, both in theoretical subjects and practical training, were by no means inferior to the boys in the group of machine workers and in that of instrument repairers.

In conjunction with the factory schools, various courses of supplementary technical training, which are attended after working hours, have played an enormous part in creating skilled women workers. During the last year of the First Five-Year Plan, women formed about a quarter of all pupils undergoing supplementary technical training in heavy industry.

The Second Five-Year Plan gave a new stimulus to technical instruction and the practical training of women workers. In 1934, 5,369 women workers of Leningrad enterprises controlled by the People's Commissariat for Heavy Industry were receiving technical instruction— a quarter of the total number of pupils. Over 2,800 women workers of the Stalin factory (Moscow) received instruction in technical circles, colleges, evening schools, and at special courses. At the Kaganovich bearing-factory, more than 1,500 women attended technical courses.

The Second Five-Year Plan witnessed a widespread national impulse among men and women workers towards full mastery of the technique of their work. A minimum standard of indispensable technical knowledge was established for every separate trade, and circles and courses were formed in all the trades for the purpose of acquiring this minimum. Workers' qualifications were overhauled, and they were obliged to pass a technical examination. Since 1935 these examinations have been obligatory for all workers in the chief branches of heavy industry. In 1936 the technical minimum was also introduced into other departments of industry. In 1935, about 800,000 workers in heavy industry passed the prescribed examination. Among the young workers, the women not only proved equal to the men in this respect, but also to a certain extent surpassed them.

SKILLED WORKER

In January 1936, the technical minimum examination was taken in the four chief branches of industry (machine-building, metallurgy, coal, and textile) by 55 per cent of the total number of young women workers and 54 per cent of the men. Half of the women received an " excellent " mark; among the men, the proportion of " excellents " was only 44 per cent. At the beginning of 1936, about two-thirds (61 per cent) of the total number of working women were receiving some form of technical training.

Not only among young women, but also among the old, the urge towards knowledge is enormous. This general impulse was well expressed by a fifty-four-year-old weaver of the Yartsev factory. " I'm fifty-four years old," she said, " but I want to learn; I want to become literate." In the cotton industry in the Moscow and Leningrad districts, 36,000 passed the technical minimum examination—the majority of them workers who had been engaged in industry for a long time.

Statistics in the Soviet Union have convincingly shown that the employment of women in skilled labour has proved thoroughly effective. The indices of productivity for skilled female labour, other conditions being equal, are equal to those for male labour. Much attention has been, and is being, paid to this question; and as early as 1931–33 extensive research was undertaken in a series of factories engaged in those branches of industry in which the large-scale employment of women had only recently been adopted.

To-day the figures of production revealed by this research have been superseded, particularly since the inauguration of the Stakhanovite movement at the end of 1935, but the conclusions reached regarding the relative efficiency of male and female labour have preserved their meaning even for the present time.

In the huge Electrozavod[1] factory at Moscow the immediate efficiency of male and female labour was revealed and compared by means of so-called " coefficients of the speed of work." If the time taken to complete a given task was less in practice than the " fixed time norm," the speed coefficient worked out to more than the unit, showing a heightened productivity of labour. If, on the contrary, the time taken was more than the " fixed time norm," the speed coefficient worked out to less than the unit, showing a lowered labour productivity. It was established by examination that the speed coefficient for turners (turning is the chief mechanical process in machine-construction) was 1·14 for women and only 0·98 for men. In other processes the correlation of coefficients was somewhat different. Among milling cutters, it was 0·89 for women;

[1] Electro-machine Building factory.

SKILLED WORKER

1·0 for men. In punching, 0·76 for women, 0·83 for men. For work on automatic turret lathes, 0·93 for women, 0·99 for men.

Only one general conclusion is possible from these figures—that at the Electrozavod, in the mechanical processes of metallurgy, the productivity of female labour does not in general differ from that of male. In some processes it is slightly higher, in others slightly lower, but these insignificant fluctuations only serve to indicate differences in the organisation of labour, a different degree of training among the women. In no way do they reveal any specific characteristics of female labour which distinguish it from male.

Analogous conclusions were arrived at by an examination conducted by the Ukrainian Institute of Labour in Kharkov machine-building factories: the Kharkov Electro-machine Building factory and the Hammer and Sickle factory. Research was conducted over a period of three months among 472 workers—punchers, winders, turret lathe workers, turners, ironworkers, drillers. It was found at the Kharkov Electro-machine Building factory that the average coefficient for winders (using the units employed at the Electrozavod) was 1·17 for men and 1·23 for women, so that the average wage earned by women on piecework was somewhat higher than that of the men.

In punching, the speed coefficient was 0·94 for women and 0·91 for men. On turret lathe work, the speed coefficient for women was higher than that for men—0·81 as compared with 0·79.

A study of the comparative efficiency of labour in the Hammer and Sickle factory gave somewhat different results. In all the processes examined—ironworking, turning, drilling—the speed coefficient of the women was somewhat lower than that of the men. In ironworking, it was 1·21 for women and 1·34 for men; in turning, 0·92 for women, 1·06 for men; in drilling, 0·90 for women, 0·96 for men. However, these results were chiefly due (as a study of general labour conditions at the Hammer and Sickle factory clearly showed) to the fact that the average industrial experience of the women was considerably less than that of the men. A woman, for example, might have been working for six months, a man for over a year. In general, the results obtained in the Ukrainian factories are analogous to those arrived at in the Electrozavod. They can be summarised as follows: Women engaged in work not physically harmful to them were, as a general rule in 1931–32, equally as efficient as men.

Women are not inferior to men as workers—in fact, they are sometimes superior to them, not only in quantitative but also qualitative indices for output. In many processes, defects are less frequent in their work than in men's. Thus, in the Karl Marx factory, in January 1932, men drillers showed a percentage of defective work of 5·3; women 0·35; among milling cutters the percentages were 2·5 for men and 0·92 for women. This is doubtless due to greater accuracy and discipline among the women. They are more careful of the objects used in their work—particularly of machines and work-benches. Here they reveal psychological characteristics developed by centuries of painstaking domestic work, with its strict economy in using up every trifle. The vast domestic experience of Soviet women is now being turned to good account in outstanding work of national importance.

Moreover, an investigation made in 1931–32 showed not only that the Soviet woman worker produced as much in a definite unit of time as a man, but also that she had learnt to exploit her working day just as fully as he. Sometimes, it was shown, she even excelled him in loading the working day to its full capacity with productive work.

In the Rostov Agricultural Machinery factory, a typical mass machine-building factory, the woman turner in 1932 spent 91 per cent of her working day in useful work: the man worker 85 per cent. Among milling cutters, the percentage for women was 87·3, for men 84·0; among planers, 85·8 for women and 81·9 for men. Loss of time through fault of the worker was in all processes considerably less among women than among men.

In the January Uprising factory in Odessa (heavy machine-building) a somewhat different state of things was revealed. In certain processes women made fuller use of their working day: among turners, the percentage for women was 90, for men 77; among modellers, 97 for women, 93 for men; among markers-off, 98 for women, 92 for men; among welders, 77 for women, 74 for men. In ironworking, press-work, drilling, and rod-work, men and women made equal use of the working day. Among milling-cutters, bolt-cutters, and some others, women gave slightly lower indices for the working day than men.

And what is particularly characteristic of the woman worker is the fact that, even in those instances where she was somewhat behindhand in exploiting her working day, the loss of time through her own fault was, as a general rule, less than with the man. This clearly shows a higher level of discipline among working women. Backwardness, when it occurs, can be explained by inadequate training. Without full mastery of the technique of her work the woman is naturally obliged to waste time in receiving instructions,

SKILLED WORKER

in getting ready for work, in regulating and repairing her tools, and in adjusting the instruments.

In the exploitation of the working year the Soviet woman worker is similarly not inferior to the man. In several instances—even in a majority—she is his superior. A study of this question in the Ural Machine-Building factory in 1931 showed that the average index for the exploitation of the working year by women almost coincided with that of the men.

In the Fighter Machine-Building factory in Moscow, women worked 89·4 per cent of all the working time in July 1931; workers in general, 90 per cent. Corresponding figures in the Karl Marx factory (Leningrad) for one summer and one winter month of 1932 are 87·5 per cent for women, 84·6 per cent for workers in general. In the October Revolution factory in Odessa, the loss of working time was less among the women than among the men for several years. In 1930, it was 7·2 per cent for women as compared with 12·1 per cent for men; in 1931, 7·4 per cent as compared with 13·4 per cent for men; in 1932, 6·9 per cent as compared with 11·6 per cent for men; in January 1933, 2·2 per cent compared with 9·4 per cent for men.

These figures must be acknowledged as all the more creditable to women because a certain considerable general loss during the working year is accounted for by the sixteen weeks' obligatory leave for pregnancy and child-bearing. This specifically feminine loss of time is in almost all instances compensated for by smaller losses for other reasons—notably for " going on the spree."

In the October Revolution factory, unjustifiable absences among women for the entire period 1930–33 constituted 0·9–0·2 per cent of the total number as compared with 2·4–0·4 per cent among the men; and similar proportions were revealed in a number of other factories—the Fighter, Karl Marx, etc.

Interesting material regarding industrial discipline and the use of the working year was collected in 1932 in the coal industry. A questionnaire sent by the Makeev Institute to a large number of mine managements in the Don Basin revealed a favourable attitude on the part of managers and technical workers towards the employment of women. The Stalin mine managers, for example, noted that women paid more attention to their work, and were more careful with machines. The working year of the women workers in all the shafts under observation was as fully exploited as that of the men. Similar results were obtained for metallurgy, the oil and timber industries, and many others.

Women as a rule change their place of work

less frequently than men; the labour turnover for women is less than that for men. In 1932, for example, the average monthly turnover in the most important workshops of the Electrozavod was 3·4 per cent for women and 5·1 per cent for men; and investigation in a number of other machine-building, metallurgical, chemical, and wood-working factories revealed much the same state of affairs. On sixteen different railway lines, 4·9 per cent of the women left work in January 1932, and 5·7 per cent of the men. The figures for July 1932 were 5·0 per cent for women, 5·7 per cent for men.

During the years 1933–35—that is, since the widespread investigation into the output of women workers that has already been described—Soviet women achieved further striking successes in technical accomplishment and the improvement of their qualifications. It is clear that these successes were, in their turn, largely responsible for a further increase in the productivity of female labour; and that where there had been earlier a certain backwardness in the efficiency of women's work as compared with men's, that backwardness was overcome. This is convincingly proved by a comparison of wages among men and women in the same categories and doing the same work at the end of 1934. In machine-building, women's earnings are almost equal to men's; in some cases they are more. In the textile industry, and others where the experience of the women is no less than that of the men, women's earnings are equal to those of men with corresponding qualifications; indeed, they somewhat exceed them. In the cotton industry in October 1934, women weavers on automatic looms earned 16·5 per cent more than men, and on mechanical looms, 3·0 per cent more.

Very characteristic of women's work in Soviet industry are the frequent examples of extraordinarily rapid promotion. It often happens that a woman who has entered industry as an unskilled labourer develops in a few years into an independent skilled worker whose outstanding industrial and social work soon earn her Union-wide fame. Here are some of these women:

In a letter sent to Stalin in January 1934, Leningrad women workers reveal that one of the shops of the Red Putilov factory was responsible for the timely delivery to the Tula factory of a 12,000-kilowatt turbine the construction of which demanded an enormous amount of complex and accurate work. This was undertaken by a brigade led by Ivanova and Shakhnovskaya and carried out in such an exemplary manner that the turbine was set up in contract time. In 1931 Ivanova was merely an unskilled labourer in the same factory.

SKILLED WORKER

Vera Bragina of the Bobriki factory was until quite recently a domestic worker in Moscow. On learning that a large factory was being built near her native village, Bobriki, she went back and started work as an unskilled labourer. In addition, she began to work steadily at improving her qualifications; took introductory training courses; then a course in mechanics. After that, she was transferred to construction work on an ammoniac factory; and three years after her arrival at Bobriki she began to work as compressor. As one of the most active shock-workers she was awarded the Order of the Banner of Labour for exemplary work.

No less significant is the history of the Ivanov textile worker, Claudia Buikova. In 1926 she came to Ivanovo from the country, quite illiterate. The labour exchange sent her to the Felix Dzerzhinsky factory as an unskilled labourer. There she soon came to the fore. In 1927 she was transferred to the factory workshop as a spool-winder. Simultaneously she studied hard to become literate and took a technical course. In a short time she became brigadier of the department in which she worked, and so distinguished herself as a worker that she received twenty-six special awards. On the fifteenth anniversary of the Komsomol[1] the Government

[1] Young Communist League.

awarded her the Order of Lenin for outstanding work.

Many such examples might be cited from the records of the First and Second Five-Year Plans. They all testify to the exceptional successes of Soviet women in skilled labour new to them—successes that are due both to Governmental policy and also to the growing social and industrial consciousness of the women themselves.

The raising of the technical level of Soviet women workers was most strikingly reflected in the Stakhanovite movement. There is an ever-increasing number of women Stakhanovites. In October 1935, only 3·0 per cent of all employees, men and women, in the cotton industry were Stakhanovites; on February 1, 1936, a fifth of all the workers (19·8 per cent) had joined the movement, and, by taking on a greater number of looms, had considerably increased their individual output. Without the mass training of workers, the range of the Stakhanovite movement would be quite unthinkable.

The initiator of the Stakhanovite movement in the textile industry was E. Vinogradova, a weaver of the Nogin factory in Vichuga who graduated from a factory school and afterwards, while working, continued to improve her qualifications. She is now considered to be the best worker in the Soviet Union, and her example teaches thousands of other textile workers, both men and women. She and her shift partner, M. Vinogradova, both work 216 automatic weaving-looms simultaneously.

Their chief rival, T. Odintsova of the Rodnikov Bolshevik Combinat, has caught up with them. In 1930 she graduated from the textile factory school; but, not content with this, she took a further technical course and passed her technical minimum examination with an "excellent" mark. At the present time she too works 216 looms.

Among the numerous pupils of E. and M. Vinogradova, E. Illarionova, a weaver of the October Revolution factory, has recently come to the fore. Illarionova works a slightly smaller number of looms than E. and M. Vinogradova and T. Odintsova—210—but she produces 4–6 per cent more cloth than they. On the first day of working 210 looms, December 1, 1935, she produced 2,807·5 metres of cloth without a single defective centimetre—a world record in weaving which stands to the present day.

Determined study and the passing of the technical minimum examination usually precede and make possible the achievements of the Stakhanovites. The initiators of the Stakhanovite movement are workers who have graduated from the factory schools and passed the technical minimum

WOMAN AS A SKILLED WORKER

with an " excellent " mark. At the Trekhgorny factory, the spinner Denisova, after passing the examination, progressed from minding four machines to eight; spinner Egorova from six to ten; weavers Pavlova, Guskova, and Lukashova—working on Platt looms—from eight to ten.

An enormous number of similar examples may be found in other branches of industry. Women workers decorated with the orders of the U.S.S.R. and women who have received certificates of merit may be found on the railways and on the sites of new constructions. There were twenty-one women among the workers decorated for building the Moscow Metropolitan Railway (Metro).

Thus, statistics of the participation of women in skilled labour and the biographies of outstanding women workers alike testify to the fact that Soviet women have firmly entrenched themselves in the most varied departments of our national activity. Contingents of skilled women workers have become established in every kind of work. Women workers are by no means inferior to men in individual output—and, in fact, often surpass them in this respect. The achievements of the women Stakhanovites show what enormous possibilities as workers are inherent in these masters of a new technique—our Soviet women, now liberated and entered into their cultural heritage.

CHAPTER IV

WOMEN IN COLLECTIVISATION

COLLECTIVISATION—the organisation of small backward individual peasant holdings into large-scale collective agricultural enterprises—is one of the outstanding achievements of the Soviet Union.

To-day, as a result of remarkable successes in the organisation of national activity during the First Five-Year Plan and the first years of the Second Five-Year Plan, and following the mass collectivisation of the countryside, agriculture has definitely entered on a new stage of development; and the collective farm has become the chief means for organising peasant production and labour.

It has already been said that by the beginning of 1936 about 90 per cent of the peasant holdings had been organised into collective farms. This has made for profound changes in the character of village culture and in the general mode of life in the villages.

"The old village, with its church in the most prominent place, with the best houses for the policeman, the priest, and the kulaks in the foreground, and with the semi-dilapidated huts of the peasants in the background, is beginning to disappear," said Stalin at the Seventeenth Party Congress. "Its place is being taken by the new village, with its public buildings, its club, radio, cinema, schools, library, crèches; with its tractors, combines, threshing-machines, and automobiles. The once important personages of the villages, the kulak-exploiters, the blood-sucking usurers, the profiteering merchant, the 'little father' policeman, have disappeared. Now the prominent personages of the village are the leading workers in collective farms and soviet farms and in the schools and clubs; the head tractor and combine driver; the leading men and women in the fields and in stock-raising farms; and the best shock-brigade workers on the collective farm fields."[1]

Collectivisation has been responsible for a particularly profound change in the position of women. Here it was faced by especially difficult problems the solution of which was of importance for its further development and consolidation. In Tsarist Russia the peasant woman was

[1] Stalin, Report on the Seventeenth Party Congress, in *Socialism Victorious*, pp. 49–50.

COLLECTIVISATION

doomed to the most humiliating servility. Exhausting work in the fields and market gardens; care of the cattle; work for her family; complete subordination to the head of the house, her husband; constant blows; almost complete illiteracy; an extremely low level of development; general oppression—this was the peasant woman's unhappy lot in the old Russia.

Soviet rule, and collectivisation, has completely changed the life of the peasant woman. She has the same civil and political rights as man; and collectivisation has given her economic independence. In the collective farms, women are paid the same rates as the men, according to the amount of work done. Collectivisation, for the first time in history, has granted the peasant woman a cultured and well-to-do life.

How do women participate in collectivisation and in work on the collective farms?

A limited degree of employment of women on the collective farms and marked seasonal disparity in this respect were characteristic of the period 1930–32. During this period, women were employed on the collective farms during the busy months (sowing and harvesting)—at first to the extent of 20–30 per cent; later (in 1932) up to 40 per cent. Researches conducted in 1931 in six collective farms in the former Central Black Soil Region show that in each of the five summer months 16–17 per cent of the annual outlay was expended on female labour; and in each of the four winter months only 0·4–1·3 per cent.

This seasonal disparity may be explained by the fact that at this period women were chiefly employed in work in the fields and market gardens—which is seasonal work. In the fields, women helped in weeding and harvesting, principally as unskilled labourers. In 1932, women were very rarely employed in mechanical ploughing or any other kind of mechanised work that was new to agriculture and required special training.

In the Black Soil Regions of the Soviet Union in 1931 and 1932, only a small number of women were employed in another important branch of agriculture—stock-raising. Even in dairy-farming they played a minor part, and were employed in the majority of collective farms only to a very limited extent. Cattle were looked after entirely by men; and there were almost no women engaged in the preparation of agricultural produce for market (grinding, etc).

Thus, in 1930–32, women were employed chiefly at the height of the season and in unskilled and semi-skilled labour. Their participation in book-keeping and the administrative work of the farms was altogether negligible. In different collective farms it varied between 2 per cent and

COLLECTIVISATION

8 per cent of the total number of such workers.

The years 1934–35 witnessed profound changes in the employment of women on the collective farms. During these years the farms continued to develop both quantitatively and qualitatively. They consolidated their economic position by mastering a new mechanised technique in agriculture and by introducing new methods of organising work: they produced at the same time vast contingents of trained workers, tractor and combine drivers, members of " shock brigades," live-stock farmers, etc.

These changes brought about a profound change in the attitude towards the employment of women. First of all, the number of women who came to work on the collective farms increased tremendously. In 1934–35 they no longer constituted 20–40 per cent of the whole, as in 1930–31, but 80–85 per cent. This sharp rise was largely the result of the exceptionally successful organisation of communal services for the benefit of workers on collective farms. Millions of children were looked after in seasonal crèches and kindergartens organised during the busy months of the year (March to September). During this same season, communal meals were provided on a vast scale in collective and soviet farms. The range of this work may be deduced from the fact that during the agricultural season of

1935 over 1,000,000 cooks were employed in field-kitchens throughout the Union.

The increase in the number of women working on the collective farms was accompanied by an increase in their output. In 1933 the daily output of a woman worker on a collective farm was 0·87 of a work-day; in 1934, 0·95; and in 1935, 0·99.[1] The resultant increase in wages among women was due on the one hand to an increase in the productivity of their labour, on the other to their promotion to more highly skilled work.

There has been a marked change in the kind of work performed by the woman farm-worker during recent years. As has been stated, the collective farms are being technically re-equipped and thoroughly mechanised. During the last four years, the number of tractors has increased threefold; on January 1, 1936, it reached 379,500, as compared with 125,300 on January 1, 1932, and 26,700 on October 1, 1928, at the beginning of the First Five-Year Plan period. During this period, agriculture has also been supplied with 46,000 combines.

Consequently the nature of agricultural labour in the Soviet Union is changing. New machines and new professions have become the

---

[1] A work-day is the unit established in the collective farms for measuring different kinds of work.

COLLECTIVISATION

deciding factors in agriculture. Trained workers predominate—tractor-drivers, combine-drivers, workers on trailers, repair mechanics, etc. All work of this kind is more or less industrial in character, and was entirely unknown in the old villages. In recent years, a veritable army of new-style workers has made its appearance in the Soviet Union. At the beginning of 1935, 550,000 tractor drivers, 64,000 combine drivers, 68,000 motor drivers, 70,000 tractor brigadiers and mechanics, were at work on collective and soviet farms. And only yesterday these 750,000 trained workers, now in charge of complicated machines, were ordinary peasants with no knowledge of skilled mechanical work. The army of new workers was trained by the widespread educational courses and schools of different types that are now in being on the collective and soviet farms and at the machine and tractor stations. In 1935, 943,800 members of collective farms, and 46,300 workers on soviet farms, were trained by these schools and courses; and these figures do not include courses for administrative work, book-keeping, etc.

The woman worker on the collective farm was, until quite recently, employed almost exclusively as unskilled labour. To-day, she has won a definite place for herself in the new ranks of qualified agricultural workers. As early as the beginning of 1933, according to incomplete figures, there were 7,000 women tractor drivers in the collective farms of the Soviet Union. Since then, this number has grown by leaps and bounds. Thus there were only 28 women tractor-drivers in the 41 machine and tractor stations of the Moscow district in 1933; by 1934 this number had risen to 147. In 1933 there were 678 women tractor-drivers in the Azov-Black-Sea district; in 1934 there were 1,260. Two or three years ago there were no women combine-drivers. At the present time—January 1, 1936—more than 500 women (6·3 per cent of the total number of combine-drivers) employed on collective farms are employed in this capacity in 573 machine and tractor stations.

These achievements did not come easily to women. They demanded persistent study. In the Voronezh district alone, 2,000 women brigadiers, 1,981 assistant brigadiers, and 3,524 detachment leaders were undergoing instruction in 1933–34. In the same district, 2,000 women were trained as chairmen of collective farms and 500 as brigadiers during the winter of 1934–35. Women are being widely trained for all kinds of mechanical work. In the same Voronezh district, 2,855 women were trained as tractor-drivers in 1934–35.

The greatest difficulty with which women had

to contend in taking up these new kinds of skilled work was men's lack of confidence in their ability to drive a tractor, keep a machine in order, and so on. Nor was this attitude only prevalent among the men. Many women, especially the older ones, considered such work " not a woman's business." Practical experience, however, has destroyed this prejudice. As early as 1933 and 1934 many women displayed outstanding ability as drivers of tractors and combines and in other responsible work. Often they were quite as efficient as the men. In the agricultural campaign of 1934, there were several occasions when outstanding brigades of women tractor-drivers took backward brigades of men " in tow " and taught them how to work.

As an example of such outstanding achievement, one can point to V. M. Barondina, mechanic of the tractor brigade of the Talovsky machine and tractor station in Western Siberia. In 1926, she became a member of a collective farm, and until 1931 worked as an ordinary labourer. In 1931, she graduated from the tractor-driving courses as a senior tractor driver. " People laughed at me," she said at the Second Congress of Collective Farm Workers, " but in the very first spring campaign I over-fulfilled the established norm. Instead of a norm of 188 hectares, my tractor ploughed 360 and took first place among all the tractors in the district.

"After this, in 1932, I was appointed brigadier of the No. 2 women's brigade. When we arrived at the collective farm for the sowing campaign —I and nine other girls—the management was very put out and quite frightened. The chairman got it into his head that his farm was in for a bad time. But in the first five days we did so much work that we were put on the red board of honour, and we carried out the plan for the sowing campaign to the extent of 110 per cent. After this we were sent to a tight spot. We put things right there, and were afterwards awarded the district red banner.

"Then I graduated from a mechanic's course, and I was given eighteen tractors and nine combines belonging to nine collective farms to look after. Here again we over-fulfilled the plan and once more were inscribed on the red board."

Barondina is not only an excellent worker, she is also an outstanding social organiser and has therefore been elected to the All-Union Central Executive Committee, the supreme organ of the Soviet Government.

In 1933 and 1934 it became evident that more women had taken up live-stock farming, and that their work was of an extremely high standard. Instead of looking after 15 cows, many milkmaids began to take charge of 27 without in any way neglecting the animals. During these years, women also became the central figures in live-stock farming on soviet farms. The number of women employed in state live-stock farms increased from 124,900 in 1932 to 302,300 at the beginning of 1935.[1]

In the Soviet Union, woman's conquest of new branches of agriculture and new kinds of skilled work, and the increase in the number of women employed in the collective farms, were accompanied by a noticeable development of social initiative among them.

As early as 1933, the women employed on the collective farms of the North Caucasus wrote to Stalin: " Now we understand where the collective farms are leading us, and what they mean for us. We see an enormous growth in political activity and the zest for work among collective farmers in the village which clearly shows the mass nature of women's participation in socialist competition and shock-work."

In 44 districts of the North Caucasus of a total of 110, the number of shock-workers covered by individual agreements for social competition increased from 39,000 in 1932 to 45,000 in 1933. In 1933, the number of shock-workers, members of shock brigades, was 360,700 for the whole district. In the Kiev district, the number of

[1] From *Statistics of the All-Union Central Council of Trades Unions.*

women shock-workers on the collective farms increased from 10,000 in 1932 to 45,000–50,000 in 1934. These new methods of organising labour —shock-work and socialist competition—were powerful factors in increasing the productivity of agricultural labour—as is clearly proved by the results of the agricultural campaign of 1935, when shock-work among collective farmers was elevated to a higher plane, where it merged into the mighty impulse of the Stakhanovite movement.

The year 1935 was distinguished by particularly outstanding achievements on the part of women workers on collective farms.

We have already described the famous campaign of the " five-hundreders " in the sugar-beet fields who, in 1935, produced a hitherto inconceivable harvest of sugar-beets—500 centners per hectare as compared with an average harvest of 130–132 centners per hectare. These " five-hundreders " were real heroines of labour, completely new types of humanity who could have grown up only under conditions of free collectivised labour.

The initiator of the " five-hundred " campaign, Maria Demchenko, was born in a poor peasant family. She was a girl of unusual talent, and, after graduation from an agricultural course, quickly came to the fore among outstanding organisers in socialist agriculture. In 1934 her detachment gathered a harvest of 469 centners per hectare. At the Second Congress of Collective Farm Shock-Workers in February 1935, Maria Demchenko pledged herself to achieve a harvest of not less than 500 centners per hectare. She and her detachment kept this promise. But it was not easily kept. In the spring there were frosts which destroyed half the seedlings; in the summer there was a drought—no rain fell for 106 days; then the harvest-fly came to destroy the beets. But persistent and undaunted labour and a knowledge of agronomics overcame all obstacles. In 1935 Demchenko and her detachment produced a harvest of 523 centners and 70 kilograms of sugar-beet per hectare.

Maria Demchenko's great service lies not merely in this outstanding achievement; it consists, above all, in the fact that she inspired many others to follow her example. Certain pupils of hers have achieved even more remarkable results than she herself. The detachment of the sixteen-year-old Hannah Shvidka produced a harvest of 576 centners per hectare, and that of the sixty-four-year-old Anna Kosheva 670 centners. Hundreds of collective farmers from the beet-growing districts either come to Demchenko for advice or write to her. In her answers, Demchenko emphasises the importance of agronomical science in the fight for record harvests. " Without science you will never get a plentiful harvest of beets, nor will they contain much sugar. Work devotedly for the good of your collective farms, develop a taste for agronomics, and things will go well with you," she writes in her answering letters. The " five-hundreders " not only draw on the science of agronomics as it is now understood, but suggest modifications to it which cannot be overlooked. Professor Karnenko, before publishing a new edition of his book *On Beet Farming*, subjected it to the criticism of the local " five-hundreders," and incorporated in it many of their corrections and suggestions.

Many outstanding workers and organisers have emerged from the ranks of women employed on the collective grain farms. At the Second All-Union Congress of Collective Farm Shock-Workers, Pasha Angelina, known throughout the Union as the organiser of women's tractor brigades, delivered a speech. When she organised her first brigade of women tractor-drivers in 1932 the collective farms were frankly incredulous: they could not believe that women were able to drive complicated machines. But the girls threw themselves heart and soul into their work. First of all they studied every detail of their tractors, and learnt how to drive them perfectly. They all passed the " technical minimum " examination with an " excellent " mark.

COLLECTIVISATION

The results were not slow in making themselves shown. The brigade began to fulfil, and more than fulfil, its allotted plan. All the collective farms in the district began to invite it to come and teach the men how to work. Pasha Angelina's brigade took first place in the All-Donets competition for tractor-drivers, and, afterwards, first place in the All-Ukrainian competition. At the Second Congress of Collective Farm Workers, this brigade promised to plough 1,200 hectares per tractor (the average norm for a tractor in terms of general ploughing work was 405 hectares for 1936 and 410 for 1935). The brigade more than carried out its promise; for each tractor ploughed the vast area of 1,225·5 hectares.

It is characteristic of Pasha Angelina that she is concerned not only with breaking records. Like Maria Demchenko, she is an ardent propagandist for her methods of work. She has taught several courses of tractor drivers, and hundreds of women who earlier had no idea of how to handle an engine have become tractor-drivers, brigadiers of tractor-brigades, or mechanics. In 1936 Pasha Angelina made two further pledges—the first, to plough 1,600 hectares per tractor; the second, to create ten new women's tractor brigades.

Besides mastering the technique of tractor-driving, women in the Soviet Union have become expert workers with even more complicated machines—combines. In 1935 the average norm for a combine was set up as 160–180 hectares. In the United States the average norm is 231 hectares. Leading Soviet women combine-drivers far surpassed the American norm in 1935. The Stakhanovite combine-driver, Maria Petrova (Jernov machine and tractor station of the Saratov district), covered an area of 544 hectares; Evdokia Vinnik (Uspensky machine and tractor station of the Dniepropetrovsk district) covered 481 hectares; Alexandra Pirozhkova (Orekhovo soviet grain farm of the Dniepropetrovsk district) covered 555 hectares; Maria Kozub (Neidorf machine and tractor station, Crimea) covered 453 hectares; and S. Sukhina (Solbot, Alexandrovsk machine and tractor station, Dniepropetrovsk district) covered 728 hectares. Thus we see that outstanding women workers in collective farms have surpassed the norms by three and four times on complicated machines like combines. And combines appeared for the first time on the fields of the Soviet Union only four to five years ago.

It is not only on the beet-fields that women have produced exceptional crops. The Soviet Union is the world's leading flax-producing country, and the Stakhanovite movement has been widely developed among flax-pullers. In

COLLECTIVISATION

October 1935 the initiator of this movement, Anna Vorobyeva, produced 34 kilograms per day of flax fibre instead of the established norm of 8 kilograms. Some of her disciples produced as much as from 40 to more than 70 kilograms per day. The collective farmer Rasogina produced 110 kilograms, and the farmer Rogosina 111 kilograms.

Underlying these remarkable achievements, and indeed the Stakhanovite movement as a whole, is the complete mastery of new methods of work. The collective farmer Molyakova is at the moment preparing for next year's record flax harvest. " We have thought of everything," she says; " we've discussed everything with the agronomists. We've used all the necessary chemical fertilisers. We've also chosen the soil scientifically. We've carefully sorted out the seeds so that they are without a single blemish." How far removed from the old home-made makeshifts of peasant cultivation are these new methods of work !

Increased harvests on the collective farms have considerably increased the incomes of the farmers. The average income from flax in the Kalinin district in 1935 was three times as large as that for 1934. In some collective farms it reached 2,500 roubles per household. The wages of the outstanding combine-drivers who have been mentioned earlier varied in 1935 between 2,000 and 4,000 roubles.

The year 1935 was one of great victories in the cotton-fields of the Soviet Union. The Union has never before harvested so much cotton. To a great extent we are indebted for these successes to the women cotton-growers of the Soviet eastern republics—Uzbekistan, Turkmenistan, Tadjikistan, Azerbaidzhan, Kazakstan, Karakalpaka. Side by side with the men they worked for cotton harvests unknown throughout the world until that time—harvests " which were never heard of before Soviet collectivisation " (Molotov). (The achievements of women in our eastern republics will be described later in a special chapter.)

In live-stock farming, also, Soviet women achieved remarkable successes in 1935. Women were the pioneers of the Stakhanovite movement among live-stock farmers. Nadezhda Persiantseva and Katherine Nartova, workers on the Red Dawn collective farm, initiated the movement among Soviet milkmaids. The average annual yield for cows in the European part of the Union in 1935 was 1,100 litres per cow. The milkmaids of the Red Dawn farm achieved a yield of 3,002 litres per cow. Milkmaids in other districts produced even better results. M. Y. Gadjyaeva achieved an average yield of 4,370 litres from 8 cows in 1935; E. Krauberger, of the Schoenfeld

COLLECTIVISATION

collective farm, in the German Volga republic, received 4,425 litres from each of 6 cows. Tasya Prokopyeva, of the Kholmogorsk soviet cattle farm, received from each of the cows in her charge an average yield of 6,290 litres, a record among milkmaids in the Soviet Union. There are already hundreds of milkmaids whose cows provide an annual yield of more than 3,000 litres.

In 1935 women collective farmers also established many new records in other branches of live-stock farming. The average litter for one sow in 1935 was 8 pigs; in many of the foremost piggeries a litter of 22 was obtained, and the eighteen-year-old pig-breeder Kharlanova achieved an average litter of 32 pigs from each sow. The average yield of wool from a single sheep in 1935 was 1·4 kilograms; the best sheep-breeders achieved a yield of 3·2 kilograms and more. Similar records were established in 1935 by state and collective farmers in other branches of live-stock farming.

The significance attached in the Soviet Union to these signal successes of women in agriculture is most strikingly demonstrated by the fact that 724 women workers on soviet and collective farms have been decorated with orders of the Soviet Union—marks of highest distinction and honour.

The social development of women, and the

growing initiative displayed by them in their work, are reflected not only in these remarkable records in production but also in the frequent promotion of women to administrative posts, both in organisation and production. As early as the beginning of 1933, Joseph Stalin observed that "collectivisation has promoted a large number of remarkable and talented women into administrative posts." In the following two years the ranks of women organisers in collectivised agriculture were considerably extended and strengthened. This is very strikingly shown by the following comparative figures:

	Number of women in thousands		
	1931	1934	1935
Chairmen of collective farms	1·2	6·0	7·0
Members of the administration	—	85·0	165·0
Managers of collective livestock farms	3·0	9·0	19·0
Brigadiers	12·0	28·0	50·0

In addition, there were, in 1933, 35,000 detachment leaders in the area of 940 machine and tractor stations (the total number of machine and tractor stations in 1934 was 3,326); in 1934 the number of detachment leaders had risen to 154,000.

The brigadier is the central executive figure in the collective farm—the direct organiser of all

COLLECTIVISATION

kinds of agricultural work. During a period of four years, as is shown by the above figures, the number of women brigadiers and detachment leaders has grown to four times the original figure.

As a result of this intensive growth in the number of women engaged in collective farm management, women have come to occupy extremely important posts in the administrative sectors of the collective farms. An investigation of 6,861 collective farms conducted in January 1936 furnished extremely interesting data in this connection. Women constituted the following percentages in the general body of administrative workers:

	Per cent
Among chairmen and vice-chairmen	2·7
„ managing bodies	18·2
„ managers of live-stock farms	16·3
„ brigadiers of live-stock brigades	22·1
„ brigadiers of land cultivation brigades	2·8
„ detachment leaders	67·5
„ club managers	10·5

These figures show that women predominate in the lower ranks of administrative personnel among detachment leaders; they also take a considerable part in live-stock management.

The chairman of a collective farm is usually a man, but even here women have consolidated their position. In certain districts of the Union the number of women in administrative posts greatly exceeds the average figures for the whole of the Union. Thus in the Voronezh district (in 595 collective farms) women constituted 8·6 per cent of the farm chairmen.

How do women cope with such responsible work?

We have already given many examples of excellent work among women who have emerged from the ranks of ordinary tractor-drivers, or were brigadiers of tractor brigades. Similar examples can be found over and over again.

Collective farms for breeding and selling stock —that is, cattle, poultry, and cows—are an enormously important factor both in agricultural life and in the life of the country as a whole; and remarkable successes have been achieved during recent years in the development of collective stock-breeding farms. The number of farms breeding cattle in the Soviet Union increased from 9,000 in 1931 to 70,000 in 1934—an increase of 7·5 times in three years. Pig-breeding farms are being developed at the same rate.

Now, women brought with them into the collective and state farms enormous experience in the care of cattle, which in peasant farming was almost always left to them. This in no small measure contributed to the development of stock-breeding in the collective farms.

One can produce innumerable examples of how

well women cope with responsible work in farm management. At the Second All-Union Congress of Collective Farm Workers, Yakovlev, director of the Agricultural Department of the Central Committee of the Party, described one of the outstanding women in live-stock farming:

" She belongs to the Red October farm in the northern district. Her name is Fomina. In 1927 her husband died and left her with two small children and a mother-in-law aged ninety. Up to 1930 she washed linen for the Kholmogorsk kulaks and then became a member of a collective farm. Here she worked as a milkmaid. Within a year she was made head milkmaid. In 1932 she was appointed brigadier, and, in 1933, manager of a farm for cattle-breeding. When she began to work in the farm in 1930 there were only 40 cows; now there are 130. These are the sort of Russian women who have entered the collective farms." Fomina herself says that at first she encountered difficulties; but the chief of them were overcome, and now every year things become better and easier.

No less striking an example is provided by A. H. Grishina, manager since 1933 of the pig farm attached to the Tractor collective farm in the Kirov district. This farm was started by the purchase of two pigs of English stock; to-day it has 120 pigs, 42 of them sows. In 1934 the sows gave birth to 560 pigs, of which 528 survived. This farm no longer buys breeding pigs; it sells them. In 1934 it sold 480 pigs. For outstanding work the farm was awarded a prize of 2,000 roubles by the district administration. A. H. Grishina has received no less than eight prizes in the course of her work.

The remarkable success of women in various branches of collective farm management has led to their promotion to administrative posts in the general management of the collective farms; as members of the managing bodies, as chairmen and vice-chairmen. Instances of such promotion, as we have already seen, have become more frequent during recent years; and the experience of these years has shown that women elected to the post of chairmen are practically always able to cope with this extremely difficult and responsible work.

V. A. Ukrainskaya, chairman of the Path to Lenin collective farm, succeeded in a very short time in extending and improving the work of the farm. She organised the breeding and selling of dairy stock, increased the number of cows reserved for the individual needs of members of the collective farm, organised two crèches and a children's playground. Under her management, seventy peasants' huts were electrified, and forty-five homes were fitted with wireless.

COLLECTIVISATION

K. I. Sitnikova, chairman of the Yakovlev collective farm in the district served by the Orlovsky machine and tractor station, was also successful in putting a badly organised farm to rights. Crops were harvested in the allotted time, implements repaired, a large granary and shed built, a piggery organised, and so on.

The work of women in the collective farms vividly illustrates the words of V. I. Lenin: "There is no doubt that there is far more organising talent among the working women and peasant women than we are aware of—people who are able to organise in a practical way and enlist large numbers of workers."[1]

All these diverse successes on the part of women farm-workers are based on their exceptional technical and cultural development, and we shall speak in detail of the achievements of the woman collective farmer in this sphere in special chapters describing the living conditions and the social and cultural development of Soviet women. Here we shall limit ourselves to general statistics showing the profound changes in the everyday life on the collective farm and in the life of the women in particular.

At the present time, illiteracy is being done away with in the remotest corners of the Union. Educational courses have been introduced

[1] Lenin, *Selected Works*, vol. ix, "A Great Beginning," p. 441.

everywhere, and the women workers on collective farms are flooding the middle and higher schools —seven-year schools, technical schools, Rabfaks (workers' schools), and universities.

More than 18,500,000 children attended seven-year schools in the villages during 1935-36, whereas in Tsarist Russia there were only 7,800,000 pupils in the primary and middle schools, both in town and country. And is not the fact that, of 60,400 clubs in the Soviet Union in 1933-34, 50,900 were in the countryside, a clear indication of the growth of culture in the Soviet village? Of these clubs, 34,200 were reading-rooms, 16,700 collective farm clubs. Similarly, in 1934 there were considerably more cinema outfits in the villages than in the towns. On January 1, 1934, there were 17,600 in the countryside, as compared with 9,900 in the towns.

The Soviet village is covered by a net of educational institutions, and, in addition, life on the collective farm is so organised that it enables women to enjoy, for the first time, all the benefits of a cultured life. The peasant woman in Tsarist Russia was illiterate and ignorant, not only because there were neither books, schools, nor any form of artistic entertainment in the old-time villages, but also because she was handicapped by poverty. Summer and winter alike she had to

COLLECTIVISATION

struggle for a piece of bread, with not a moment's leisure for other things.

Collectivisation has given the woman complete equality and economic independence; it has lightened her lot and created the conditions necessary for a cultured, well-to-do life. These facts emerge very clearly when we compare the daily time-table of the woman worker on a collective farm with that of a peasant woman in the period preceding general collectivisation.

Widespread investigations of how workers utilise their time are sometimes conducted in the Soviet Union. In agriculture such investigations were carried out in 1923 and 1934. The results show that in 1923, when the lot of the peasant woman was already considerably less burdensome than in Tsarist Russia, she nevertheless worked under great strain in the fields during the busy season. In 1923 a married peasant woman spent in the summer a daily average of 16 hours (15 hours 51 minutes) on agricultural and domestic work. She regularly went short of sleep. About $5\frac{1}{2}$ hours (5 hours 43 minutes) of the twenty-four went on sleep and $2\frac{1}{2}$ hours on rest.

The time-table of a worker on a collective farm in the summer of 1934 is different. The working day has been shortened by 2 hours 45 minutes, and thus lasts about 13 hours; this includes 6 hours of agricultural work. There is practically an hour's more sleep and nearly two hours (1 hour 53 minutes) more for rest and cultural work. The arrangement of the peasant woman's winter day shows a less marked change. The time spent on work has been shortened by one hour—from 12 hours 17 minutes to 11 hours 15 minutes; consequently there is more time for sleep and rest. These comparative figures show how the life of a woman engaged in agriculture has been made easier. Her work has been cut down and her leisure almost doubled. A shorter working day has given the woman farm-worker time for study, for social work, for improving her living conditions.

All these changes are indicative of the gradual disappearance of the difference between town and country in the Soviet Union. This is chiefly the result of technical and economic changes in Soviet agriculture—the industrialisation of agriculture, its mechanisation and electrification; the organisation of machine and tractor stations and of different services on the collective farms, such as repair shops, etc. The development of culture in the villages is to a great extent dependent on these factors. And the woman worker on the collective farm played from the very beginning a leading rôle in the historic upheaval that was directed towards abolishing the

COLLECTIVISATION

antithesis between town and country. By their work in collectivised agriculture the vast masses of women farm-workers have become a mighty social force.

As has been already emphasised, soviet farms were just as important in the reorganisation of agriculture in the Soviet Union as collective farms. These large soviet agricultural enterprises are indeed " schools for teaching new methods of work and nurseries for every kind of technical improvement and innovation which, after first being tried out in the soviet farms, are then applied generally on a vast scale in the collective farms."

We find the same tendencies in the soviet farms with regard to the employment of women as in other agricultural enterprises. The number of women on state farms increased $3\frac{1}{2}$ times during the years 1928–35—from 334,000 to 1,123,000 (including temporary and seasonal workers). On July 1, 1935, women constituted 40·3 per cent of the total number of workers. The proportion of women among trained workers (among the permanent contingents of soviet farm-workers) is increasing rapidly. In September 1935 women constituted 13·5 per cent of the brigadiers working in the fields and 17 to 36 per cent (according to the different kinds of stock) of the brigadiers in live-stock farming.

WOMEN IN COLLECTIVISATION

Women workers on soviet farms, as well as those on the collective farms from whose ranks they have chiefly emerged, participate widely in socialist competition and shock-work, and have produced brilliant examples of productive work. They, too, attend various educational courses, study in circles and schools, struggle to improve and refashion their mode of life. Among the outstanding agricultural workers decorated by the Government in 1935 there were many from the soviet farms.

Thus in the state farms, too, women have won for themselves a prominent and respected place in the leading ranks of workers in Soviet agriculture.

CHAPTER V

WOMAN IN THE INTELLECTUAL PROFESSIONS AND IN ADMINISTRATIVE WORK

THE ACQUISITION of technical skill is only the first step in becoming a qualified worker. Afterwards come those qualifications that are connected with one or other of the functions of leadership—the work of specialists, engineers and technicians; of foremen in industry and transport; of agronomists in agriculture. In this group may be included the medical, legal, and financial professions, economists, and all kinds of scientific workers.

These types of workers chiefly receive their training from the middle schools and universities which specialise in fitting them for different professions. But there are also in all branches of business and industry large numbers of highly skilled workers who have risen from the ranks without any special education. The Soviet Government creates favourable conditions for the

IN THE PROFESSIONS

work of these men and women, and provides special instruction which gives them theoretical training. The ranks of specialists turned out by the training schools largely consist of former workers who form a very strong group among Soviet students.

What is the part played by women in these intellectual professions? Are they to be found in the ranks of engineers and technicians, in leading industrial and administrative posts? And, above all, what provision is there in the middle and higher schools for training women for these appointments?

In Tsarist Russia, higher education was almost completely closed to women; only after 1905 was there some improvement, and then only in certain branches of education. At the beginning of the twentieth century there were only three high schools for women: St. Petersburg Women's Courses with literary, historical, and mathematical faculties; Moscow Courses of the same type; and a Women's Medical Institute in St. Petersburg. During the revolutionary years of 1905–06 the net of women's advanced courses was spread more widely. As well as in the capitals (Moscow and St. Petersburg), courses were organised in important provincial centres—Odessa, Kharkov, Kiev, Kazan, and others. The number of pupils increased. In 1909 there were

AND ADMINISTRATIVE WORK

5,770 women studying at the advanced courses in St. Petersburg. But the majority of the newly provided courses taught exactly the same subjects as the older institutions, and gave women access only to pedagogical work, or, to a limited extent, to medicine. About this time, however, some courses were organised in entirely new fields—two juridical and two agricultural (Moscow and Leningrad).

It must further be emphasised that in Tsarist Russia these advanced courses were possible only to women of means. For workers and peasants, and even for wide strata of the bourgeoisie, the tuition was prohibitively expensive. As a result, women's participation in the intellectual professions was, in Tsarist Russia, chiefly confined to pedagogical work; and the more so because teaching was very badly paid, and it was therefore easier for women to secure posts as teachers. A large number of women were engaged in teaching in the large towns. In Moscow in 1912 there were 10,500 thus employed —64 per cent of the town's teachers; but the mass of women taught in the primary elementary schools.

Of doctors of all types, women in Moscow constituted 15 per cent in 1912; of the lower medical personnel, 70 per cent were women. A fairly large number of women were employed

IN THE PROFESSIONS

in keeping accounts, chiefly in the less qualified posts. The presence of women in the intellectual professions that required special training was, in Moscow in 1912, altogether negligible. In the provinces, women were to be found even more rarely in such professions than in the capitals, which were the only centres—and miserable centres at that—of specialised training for women.

During the war, 1914-15, women were more frequently employed in the intellectual professions, owing to the mass mobilisation of men; but even at this period they were confined to the same spheres of activity as before.

A radical change in this state of affairs took place after the formation of the Soviet Union. The Soviet authorities abolished all restrictions against women, opened the middle and higher educational institutions to them, and did all in their power to attract them into these schools.

No less profound a change was made in the social composition of pupils in the universities and technical colleges. These institutions were systematically " proletarianised " for the purpose of creating, side by side with the ranks of the old specialists, a new intelligentsia drawn from workers and peasants.

In order to prepare the workers and peasants for advanced courses, a new type of educational

AND ADMINISTRATIVE WORK

institution was created—the Workers' Faculty, or " Rabfak." The Rabfaks were a tended exclusively by workers and peasants, who in a three- or four-year course received a full pre-university education; and they have played an enormous part in creating a new Soviet intelligentsia.

By the end of 1926 the number of women among the ranks of the specialists had grown considerably in comparison with the pre-war period. The figures for Moscow show this very clearly.

The number of women engaged in Moscow in cultural and educational work, particularly among teachers, remained in 1926 at about pre-war level. But among medical and nursing workers the proportion increased from 56·5 to 72 per cent, and among office and secretarial employees from 19·5 to 42 per cent.

In 1926, Soviet women already constituted a fairly large section of the main groups of administrative and technical personnel, from which they had been altogether excluded in Tsarist Russia.

By the end of 1926 there were already 16,000 women in administrative posts (8·2 per cent of the total number); 7,000 among technical personnel (4 per cent); 700 agronomists (9 per cent); 800 lawyers (5·8 per cent); and so on.

IN THE PROFESSIONS

However, the real turning-point came during the reconstruction period, and chiefly the period of the First and Second Five-Year Plans. The fulfilment of the First Five-Year Plan demanded a considerable increase in the ranks of specialists in all spheres of industry and commerce.

At the beginning and end of the Five-Year-Plan the number of specialists with higher and middle education numbered as follows:

	End 1928	Beginning 1933
National economy	146,000	375,000
Pedagogics	211,500	387,200
Medicine	135,500	211,000
	493,000	973,200

As the table shows, during the first four years of the First Five-Year Plan the number of trained workers of both sexes in administrative posts increased more than 2·5 times. Taken altogether, specialists in these fields were almost doubled by the end of the First Five-Year Plan and numbered almost a million people. If we add professions not covered by these figures, and technical workers without complete specialised training, the number rises to 2,500,000.

This growth in the ranks of specialists continues just as intensively in the period of the Second Five-Year Plan. At the beginning of 1933, engineers, technicians, and expert operatives numbered 375,000, and, in July 1935, 500,000. This enormous increase in the number of working specialists is the result of marked changes in training methods and of the reorganisation of the whole system of the middle and high schools. The number of pupils in advanced educational institutions increased from 170,000 in 1928 to 523,200 in 1935—almost threefold; the number of pupils in technical colleges from 195,000 in 1928 to 710,000 in 1935—more than threefold; the number of pupils in Rabfaks from 50,000 to 284,000—more than five and a half times as many.

During these years the number of women, both among pupils and specialists, increased even more rapidly than the general increase for both sexes. Consequently, not only the absolute number of women, but also their proportion to the general number of pupils and specialists, shows an increase. Let us examine the figures for women in the special training-schools for workers in commerce and industry.

According to the figures of the Central Administration of the National Economy statistics of the Soviet State Planning Commission, the proportion of women in the technical colleges increased from 37·6 per cent in 1928 to 44·1 per cent in 1935; and in universities from 28·1 per cent in 1928 to 39 per cent in 1935. The absolute

IN THE PROFESSIONS

number of women in the universities increased from 74,800 in 1928 to 177,300 in 1935 (more than twice as many). In the technical colleges it grew from 73,300 in 1928 to 279,700 in 1935 (almost four times as many). In the workers' faculties, women in 1928 numbered 7,700 (15·6 per cent); in 1935 this number had increased to 98,000 (36·6 per cent).

In the industrial colleges there were 48,000 women (23·3 per cent in 1935 as against 13·4 per cent in 1928); in agricultural colleges, 19,500 (31·8 per cent as against 17·4 per cent in 1928); in social-economic services, 12,100 (39 per cent as against 21·1 per cent in 1928); in pedagogics, 51,600 (48·4 per cent as against 48·7 per cent in 1928); in the medical profession, 46,100 (71·2 per cent as against 52 per cent in 1928).

In the technical colleges the proportion of women in all faculties in 1935 was even higher than in the universities. In the industrial technical colleges women constituted 29·6 per cent of the total number of pupils (as against 9·5 per cent in 1928); in the agricultural schools 32 per cent as against 15·4 per cent in 1928; in the social-economic schools, 54·6 per cent as against 36·3 per cent in 1928; in the pedagogical schools, 55·2 per cent; and in medical schools, 79·7 per cent.

AND ADMINISTRATIVE WORK

The number of women specialists in all branches of national economy grew in proportion to the growth of special training for women in all types of training institutions. For the period 1926–31 (according to the figures of the 1926 census and the town registration of 1931) the number of women in the basic groups of specialists increased at the following rate:

Profession	Number of women employed (in thousands)		Percentages of the total number of workers in the given profession	
	1926	1931	1926	1931
Legal workers	0·8	1·7	5·8	13·7
Higher technical staff	1·4	6·6	3·1	7·4
Agronomists	0·7	2·2	9·1	14·0
Technicians	0·4	6·7	1·3	8·8

This table reveals considerable progress in the employment of women as technical personnel during the period 1926–31. The number of women employed in technical posts increased 4·8 times for the higher grades and 15·5 times for the middle grades. The growth of the absolute number of women was accompanied by a sharp rise in the proportion of women in all categories of specialists.

It is interesting to note that the number of women draughtsmen increased 17·2 times—in 1926 there were very few women in this profession (13·6 per cent), but in 1931 they already

IN THE PROFESSIONS

constituted more than half the total number (50·8 per cent).

The number of women shop-managers in State business increased from 1,000 in 1926 to 7,000 in 1931, their proportion from 2·7 per cent to 10·4 per cent. There was also a marked growth in the number of women employed in office work. In Moscow, women book-keepers, accountants, and statisticians amounted to 29·7 per cent in 1926 and 43·7 per cent in 1931.

But these achievements, however striking in themselves, pale before the success of women in mastering the highly skilled work of specialists. In every branch of national activity during the years of the First and Second Five-Year Plans we find a sharp increase in the number of women specialists. In industry, in 1930, women constituted 4 per cent of the total number of specialists; at the beginning of 1934, 9·2 per cent, with an absolute increase of 11·8 times their earlier number—i.e. from 3,600 to 42,600. On July 1, 1935, there were already 66,100 women employed on the technical engineering side of heavy industry—that is, 13·7 per cent of the total number.

In transport, the proportion of women specialists increased from 1 per cent in 1930 to 4·4 per cent at the beginning of 1934, with an absolute increase in their number from 235 to

AND ADMINISTRATIVE WORK

4,400—i.e. more than eighteen times as many. In agriculture, women specialists constituted, in 1930, 5·5 per cent of the total number (2,500); at the beginning of 1934 they formed 8·9 per cent (80,000), with a more than threefold increase in the absolute number. Characteristic of the employment of women specialists in former times was their limited participation in actual practical work; for the most part they were confined to the managing department. In recent years this state of affairs has greatly altered.

The basic ranks of specialists in industrial enterprises consist of workshop personnel, engineers, foremen, technicians, and laboratory workers. Among the higher ranks of these there were only 1,700 women in 1930—3 per cent of the total number. At the beginning of 1934 there were 16,000 women specialists employed in industrial workshops—8·4 per cent of the total number. The absolute number of women in this higher category increased 9·5 times over this period, whereas the general number of workshop specialists increased only 3 to 4 times.

In the middle departments of industrial workshop management (supervisors, brigadiers) the achievements of women during these years were even more outstanding. In 1930 there were only 395 women (1·9 per cent) in this category. At the beginning of 1934 the number had risen

IN THE PROFESSIONS

to 3,440—almost nine times as many—and their percentage from 1 to 4·2.

The largest number of women is to be found on the staffs of factories engaged in light industry, where women have had most experience. In the enterprises covered by the People's Commissariat for Light Industry, 29 per cent of the specialist-operatives and 15 per cent of the supervisors were women at the beginning of 1934. In the middle of 1935, in those industries chiefly dependent on female labour, women constituted from one-fifth to a half of the total number of engineering and technical workers; in the sewing industry the proportion was 47·7 per cent; in knit-wear, 38·5 per cent; in confectionery, 32·5 per cent; in rubber goods, 27·8 per cent; in cotton, 19 per cent.

Women have been particularly successful in laboratory work. The proportion of women laboratory workers in the machine-building industry was 53 per cent in 1934 as against 11·8 per cent in 1925; in the chemical industry, 75 per cent as against 22·5 per cent in 1925. The number of women in the general ranks of engineering and technical workers in the chemical industry is also comparatively high. On June 1, 1935, it was 25·2 per cent.

We have a general striking example of women who were recently unskilled labourers but are

AND ADMINISTRATIVE WORK

now performing brilliant work as technicians and engineers. Thus, for instance, Klopotunova took part in building the Stalingrad tractor factory, carried bricks, dug, washed glasses. She was then transferred to the assembly shop and to working the machinery. As a result of persistent effort to improve her qualifications and master the technique of her work, she was promoted to the head of the mechanical assembly shop. At the present time she is assistant to the head of the laboratory, and is finishing a course at the institute for the hot working of metals.

The young technician-constructor, Hesny Nasurdinova, a Tartar, was for a time in a Tartar school, passed through the seven-year school, and took a course at a building technical college. To-day she is doing magnificent work as a technician constructor in Kazan, and is well known for her public activities. She is only twenty-two years old.

E. P. Nadeinskaya also deserves special mention. An apprentice ironworker in 1929, she became a fully fledged engineer, specialising in the cold working of metals. Her short period of work as an engineer has been distinguished by several brilliant achievements. While working in the Orgametal concern she solved the problem of putting into operation the Klinbergen machine for spiral wheels, the working of which had for a long time baffled our engineers. Recently she has been working at the Kharkov Railway engine factory as chief engineer of the assembly and repair department. In addition to this, she occupies the chair of the cold working of metals at the Stalin Industrial Academy, and her department has been put on the red board for its excellent work.

At the Dorogomilov chemical factory in Moscow there were, in 1935, 185 women engineers, technicians, and laboratory workers. Engineer Khmelnitskaya, head of the eighth section, is considered one of the best production organisers in the factory. C. Pergaments, chemist in the chief laboratory, and many other women engineers and technicians combine excellent work with splendid social activity.

Sophie Grinstein was the first woman shipbuilding engineer in the Soviet Union. She began her career as an apprentice ironworker, and now occupies the responsible post of an engineer-technician in the Leningrad Marti shipbuilding factory. The first powerful timber-carrying motor-propelled ships, *Exportles, Dvinoles, Volgales,* and *Komiles,* were built under her supervision.

The great strides made by women in mastering technical knowledge are reflected in their entry into the field of invention, where they formerly played no part whatever.

AND ADMINISTRATIVE WORK

As early as the end of 1932 there were 110,200 members of invention circles (6·4 per cent of the total number of workers) in 800 Soviet enterprises. Since then, invention in the Union has become even more widespread. In 1932 women constituted 10·6 per cent of these circles. Their share in invention is gradually growing in proportion to the increase in their technical knowledge and the growth in their numbers. In 1934 there were as many as 9,000 women inventors in Moscow alone.

A number of women inventors are now famous throughout the Union. Natalie Sholtz, a young engineer, has invented a new means of telephonic communication between towns by means of a subterranean cable. She has been put forward as a candidate for the All-Union Engineers' Roll of Honour. The rubberised jacket of the stratosphere balloon *U.S.S.S.*, a world-wide triumph for Soviet science, was made in the Kauchuk factory in Moscow under the supervision of the women engineers Kusina and Levitina, who were subsequently decorated by the Government for this work.

Many ordinary workers have shown themselves capable inventors. O. Lunina, of the Kauchuk factory; the Electrocombinat workers Nikanorova and Proletarskaya; P. Koserev, of the Volodarsky factory in Leningrad, and many others have

IN THE PROFESSIONS

been awarded the Orders of Lenin and of the Red Banner of Labour for their valuable inventions.

The number of women in other categories of the Soviet intelligentsia—among agronomists, teachers, doctors, scientific workers—has likewise grown with great rapidity.

Women specialists in agriculture numbered about 8,000 at the beginning of 1934, constituting 8·8 per cent of the total number. About 2,000 of them worked as agronomists on tractor stations, on state farms, and in land administration (10·5 per cent of the total number).

The number of women doctors in the Soviet Union has grown from 30,500 in 1931 to 42,000 in 1935. In 1914 there were only 1,900 women doctors—less than a twentieth of the present number. In 1935, women constituted almost half (48·9 per cent) of the total number of doctors as against 9·7 per cent in 1914 and 44·9 per cent in 1931. The majority of them work in the towns, particularly the large towns. In 1934 they constituted 66 per cent of the total number of doctors in Moscow (in 1912, 15 per cent). Now they form a large section (about 40 per cent) even among country doctors.

Even in the old days, as we have already shown, more than half the teachers in Russia were women, but most of them taught in the elemen-

AND ADMINISTRATIVE WORK

tary schools. To-day, women form a majority on the staffs of the town middle schools and a large proportion of the staff of the village middle schools. In the elementary schools they are still in an overwhelming majority.

Here is the growth of the proportion of women in schools for 1927–35 in percentages of the total number of teachers:

	Elementary School		Middle School	
	1927	1935	1927	1935
In the towns ..	81·3	90·2	43·6	59·8
In the villages ..	61·6	67·9	28·3	41·1

Women are widely employed in office work and form an overwhelming majority among the statisticians and accountants. In a series of industries (sewing, bootmaking) women book-keepers are in the majority. Their participation in commercial management has been greatly extended. In a fifth of all town shops the manager or assistant manager is a woman.

The frequent presence of women in the State judicial system is worth noting. At the end of 1933 they held 9·1 per cent of the total number of its posts. They work as magistrates (there were 58 women magistrates in the Russian Socialist Federative Soviet Republic in 1935) and as public prosecutors.

Particularly distinguished work has been done by Soviet women in scientific institutes and in

IN THE PROFESSIONS

advanced academic institutions. No restrictions are imposed on women in the Soviet Union in the field of independent scientific work; they can be professors, research workers, and so on. A woman submits her thesis for a doctorate and other degrees on equal terms with a man. The most advanced centres of scientific work are the Academies of Science of the U.S.S.R. and those of the Union republics of the Ukraine and White Russia. The members are chosen by annual elections, and there are no restrictions against women in these elections.

At the beginning of 1935 more than 11,000 women worked in Soviet research institutes as compared with 5,100 in 1929. Women to-day constitute 29 per cent of the total number of scientific workers (as against 22·8 per cent in 1929). They form about the same proportion of postgraduate students in research institutes. In 1935 there were 101 women scholars in the 17 research institutes of the Soviet Academy of Sciences, in which the most important scientific forces of the Union are concentrated.

Women play a considerable part in scientific pedagogical work in advanced academic institutions. Thus in 1935 they constituted 15 per cent of the total number of professors, docents, and assistants. In pedagogical colleges and universities they form almost a quarter (23 per cent) of the staff. In a number of institutes the directors and assistant directors are women.

A whole series of important scientific achievements—discoveries in all fields of theoretical knowledge and scientific practice—are linked up with the names of women. In the Tsvetmetzoloto (non-ferrous metals) State Research Institute seven women scientific workers have been decorated for their exceptionally valuable achievements. A group of women scientists—N. Bach, R. Burstein, G. Levina, F. Marshak—have conducted a series of most important experiments at the Karpov Chemical Research Institute.

One of the most outstanding Soviet engineers is C. Umova. While working in the Gipromez[1] she put forward her own design for standard blast and open-hearth furnaces in competition with the drawings of American engineers. Umova's design has considerably lowered the cost of construction, and these types of furnaces in the Soviet Union are now built according to her specifications.

In the mathematical world there is Yanovskaya, Professor of the Research Institute for Mathematics and Mechanics of the First Moscow State University, who has several works on the history and methodology of mathematics to her credit. The editing of Marx's mathematical

[1] State Institute for Planning Metallurgical Factories.

IN THE PROFESSIONS

manuscripts has recently been conducted under her supervision. In addition to research work, she lectures extensively. We must also note A. Bykhovskaya, Director of the Institute of Zoology and Dean of the Biological Faculty.

The promotion of women to leading administrative posts as directors of industrial enterprises, workshop managers, and so on, has taken on tremendous significance in the Soviet Union. Such posts are difficult, and burdened with great responsibility. Particularly high demands are made of a factory director in a period of socialist reconstruction. Naturally only the best workers, with high qualifications and great experience in their work and in public activity, are promoted to such posts.

On May 1, 1930, among all the directors of industrial enterprises, deputies, and assistants, there were only 86 women—1 per cent of the total number. But, thanks to the general cultural, political, and technical growth of women workers, and as a result of the policy of the Soviet authorities, which has been unswervingly directed towards promoting women to administrative posts, the ranks of women leaders in industry are rapidly being enlarged.

At the end of 1933, according to the figures of the Central Administration of National Economy Statistics, there were already 325 women directors

AND ADMINISTRATIVE WORK

of Soviet industrial enterprises (2 per cent of the total number). Thus in three years the number of women directors has grown three and a half times. In light industry, women constitute 8 per cent of the directors. These percentages are, of course, not very large, but they testify to an extremely important fact—that in the Soviet Union groups of women with the highest technical and administrative qualifications have been formed. These women are entrusted with the management of some of the largest enterprises in the Union, and there can be no doubt that their number will grow with the years.

Socialist construction has brought to the fore a number of women whose work is a model of administrative activity. Among these are: G. Sagaoutdinova, director of the No. 3 Krupskaya factory in Kazan (awarded the Order of the Red Banner of Labour); K. Ukolova, deputy director of the Trekhgorny textile factory in Moscow (decorated for special services with the Order of the Red Banner of Labour); T. Molotova, who rose from ordinary labourer to engineer and is now deputy-director of the Bolshoi Shuisky textile factory; Agroskina, director of the Krasnokholmsky factory in Moscow (she was awarded first prize in the directors' competition in 1934 and inscribed in the roll of honour); Kochenogova, director of the best cotton factory, the

IN THE PROFESSIONS

Krasnii Textilshchiki (Red Textile-Workers); and many others.

We have already mentioned the exceptional successes of women in agricultural administration. In other branches of national activity (transport, communications, communal restaurants, finance) we find many women successfully managing whole enterprises.

But women do not limit themselves to the management of businesses. They have penetrated to even higher places in public administration. At the beginning of 1934 they constituted 12 per cent of the specialists and managers of combines and trusts. Among chief managers, 10 per cent; in the People's Commissariats, 15·2 per cent. A woman at the head of a trust, as director of a department of a People's Commissariat, is by no means a rare occurrence. T. Smirnova, former worker in a spinning factory, now occupies the post of deputy director of the Vladimir Cotton Trust; E. Smirnova is deputy director of the Kostroma Linen Trust.

The Soviet perfume and cosmetic industry, which has developed rapidly during the last few years, is chiefly concentrated in the two trusts known as Teje and Lenjet. These enormous trusts comprise large factories, commercial enterprises, plantations, etc., and have already achieved considerable success both in increasing the quantity of their output and improving its quality. At the head of these trusts are women: Jemchuzhnina and Shaposhnikova, two of the most gifted directors in the Union. In 1936 they travelled in Europe and America in order to study the manufacture of perfumes and cosmetics. In America they were received by President Roosevelt.

The presence of women in leading positions in the People's Commissariats may be illustrated by drawing attention to a Commissariat so important in State management as that of finance. Women formerly had not even the remotest connection with problems of financial policy or management. To-day, many important posts in the Commissariats of Finance of the U.S.S.R. and of the Union republics are held by women. The People's Commissariat of Finance for the largest Soviet Republic, R.S.F.S.R., is headed by Barbara Yakovleva. In the central administration of the Commissariat of Finance of the U.S.S.R. six women are at the head of important managing departments. An extremely important department, the Budget department, is directed by A. Smilga. There are also in the Commissariat 103 women employed in leading operative posts.

There are, too, a number of women in the soviets—the highest State organs of the U.S.S.R. The percentage of women in Government administrative posts is shown in the following table:

IN ADMINISTRATIVE WORK

	1929 Per cent	1934 Per cent
Members of Village Soviets	18·8	26·8
Members of District Executive Committees	19·4	22·7
Members of the All-Russian Central Executive Committee (VTsIK)	13·5	17·5
Members of the Central Executive Committee of the Soviet Union (TsIK)	11·4	13·3

The Central Executive Committee of the U.S.S.R. has 101 women members. In Uzbekistan, where in Tsarist days women were helpless slaves, the post of deputy chairman of the Central Executive Committee is held by an Uzbek woman, Djakhan Abidova.

CHAPTER VI

TOWARDS A HEALTHIER LIFE FOR WOMEN

THERE IS A CLOSE CONNECTION between the problems that affect woman as a worker and the organisation of her everyday life. On the one hand, the absorption of women into public work postulates a fundamental reorganisation of ordinary living conditions; on the other, the very fact of women's participation in such work is a powerful factor in the refashioning of women's lives. In this sense, the mass absorption of women into production and the reorganisation of their everyday life are in fact two different aspects of one and the same process.

Woman's life is being reorganised in the Soviet Union first of all by the creation of a widespread net of communal services (crèches, kindergartens, communal restaurants) which are designed to lighten the burden of exhausting and unproductive domestic work. Thus women will have more time for work, for study, and for leisure; and only thus can the necessary conditions for reorganising the whole of life on a healthier basis be created.

The problem of releasing women from the bondage of tiresome domestic work cannot be easily solved. It is enough to point out that in 1930, when the net of communal services was already fairly well developed in the towns, the general burden of women's work, although considerably less than it had been, was still very oppressive. Working women worked four hours a day more than men, owing to the fact that practically all the domestic work was done by women.

The Soviet authorities have continually emphasised the cardinal importance of a widespread development of communal services and the close connection between this development and the mass absorption of women into industry. Thus, as early as 1930, the Council of People's Commissars of the R.S.F.S.R.[1] stated, in a decree published on the employment of women in industry and in Governmental institutions, that " insufficiency of essential communal services, particularly of crèches and kindergartens, was the chief obstacle to the mass absorption of women into production." It therefore commissioned the State Planning Commission of the R.S.F.S.R. to work out " a project for widening the net of crèches and

[1] Russian Socialist Federative Soviet Republic.

kindergartens for 1931 in order that they might fully cope with the children of working women new to industry, and also considerably extend the services afforded to women already at work."

The decree of the All-Union Central Executive Committee and the Council of People's Commissars of the R.S.F.S.R. of September 21, 1932, was of great practical significance in providing crèches in towns and industrial centres, and on state and collective farms and machine and tractor stations. It stated that " the further increased activity of women in economic and political life demands an intensive development of the net of communal services, of which the most important is the crèche."

In July 1935 the Council of People's Commissars of the U.S.S.R. published a further decree concerning the organisation of crèches and pre-school education for infants which considerably increased the amount of money allotted to these services. These facts clearly show that in the Soviet Union the organisation of communal services is considered to be a problem of primary importance, and as such receives constant attention from the Government.

What is the actual position to-day in different branches of communal service? What has the Soviet Government achieved in this sphere?

In the Soviet Union we attach enormous

significance to the communal education of infants. Apart from its obvious pedagogical advantages, the development of a communal system of infant education is of paramount importance in releasing women from the burden of domestic drudgery.

The following statistics illustrate this quite clearly. In the time-table of a married woman not engaged in industry the general amount of time spent in domestic work in 1930 was double that spent by a married woman worker; the amount of time spent by the former in looking after small children was 4·5 times that spent by the latter. This comparison shows quite clearly that the care of small children is the chief responsibility which binds a woman to domestic work.

Communal infant education, therefore, is particularly important in freeing women from family cares and allowing them to engage in work useful to society. Only thus can the standard of life be raised, not only for the women themselves, but also for their families.

The first stage in the communal education of children in the Soviet Union is the crèche. This provides children of from six weeks to three years old with the necessary physical care and social education. The crèches are divided into several age-groups, each with its own hygienic and pedagogical routine. Diet is based on scientific principles: the children sleep at regular hours and they are systematically hardened by being left out in the fresh air at all seasons of the year. The crèches also have a certain pedagogical function. They develop certain talents in the children and teach them habits which foster their social consciousness, their aptitude for work, and their love of hygiene. Before going to work, a woman will take her child to the crèche with complete confidence, because she knows that there it will find everything necessary for its normal healthy development.

Crèches in the Soviet Union may be divided into two fundamental types—permanent crèches which function the whole year round, and seasonal crèches which are set up in country districts during the busy agricultural months (spring, summer, and autumn).

How has the crèche system developed in the Soviet Union?

The table on p. 146 shows that the First and Second Five-Year Plans are distinguished by a particularly intensive development of crèche services.

Thus by 1936 more than 5,500,000 children were being looked after in some form or other of crèche (as compared with 257,000 at the beginning of the First Five-Year Plan).

Under the First Five-Year Plan the development of the crèche system was particularly

	No. of places in crèches in thousands		
	1928	1932 (end of First Five-Year Plan)	1936 (beginning)
In crèches of all types throughout the Union	257·0	4,544·3	5,631·7
(a) Town, permanent	52·4	262·7	302·6
(b) Country, all types including:	204·4	4,270·5	5,309·2
(1) permanent	6·9	350·2	436·1
(2) seasonal	197·8	3,920·3	4,873·1

intensive in agricultural districts. This was the period of mass collectivisation, when the conditions of women's life and work were being fundamentally reorganised. The number of children in country crèches increased by 26 times during the period 1928–35; in the towns it increased by 6 times. It is significant that in the national republics of the Union the growth of the crèche system was even more intensive than in the Union as a whole. At the beginning of 1935 in the Z.S.F.S.R.[1] the number of crèches had increased 55 times since 1928: in Uzbekistan 13·5 times; in Turkmenistan 80 times. The organisation of crèches in these republics belongs almost entirely to this period. In Tadjikistan there were no crèches at all in 1928; by the end of 1935 they were serving 27,600 children.

The number of young children in crèches

[1] Transcaucasian Socialist Federative Soviet Republic.

increased in proportion. In 1935 they constituted 12 per cent of all children of crèche age in the towns as compared with 2·5 per cent in 1928; in the country, during the busy season, 40 per cent as compared with 1·5 per cent in 1928.

There was a particularly noticeable increase in the number of crèches for children of industrial workers. In 1935, 80 per cent of the children of workers belonging to the miners' trade union were looked after in crèches: in the machine-building industry, 55 per cent; in metallurgy, 65 per cent; in the cotton industry, 70 per cent; in the wool industry, 70 per cent; among seamstresses, 65 per cent. The children of practically all the workers in the giant plants at Magnitogorsk, Cheliabinsk, Zlatoust, and Kabakovsk (former Nadezhdinsk), and in the Stalin factory at Moscow, are cared for in the crèches. The system has been so widely developed that for the overwhelming majority of women workers, both in town and country, there is a crèche in which they can leave their children. Women greatly appreciate the crèches because they know that in them children will receive everything necessary for normal healthy growth, while for the women themselves crèches mean freedom to work in some branch or other of national production and the possibility of developing their cultural life.

During 1931–32, the number of crèches was increased chiefly by exploiting resources ready to hand; that is, by the extension and alteration of existing premises and the use of buildings not specially equipped for the purpose. These make-shift measures naturally affected the quality of the services provided by the crèches.

From 1933 onwards, the practice of planning and constructing special buildings for crèches was widely adopted. In 1935, 120 new crèches were built in collective farms of the Bashkirian Autonomous Republic; 125 in the Kuibishev district; and 69 in the Tartar republic. In Stalinsk, the mighty industrial centre which has grown up in Siberia during the last five years, and now has over 100,000 inhabitants, the best-built, best-equipped house is the crèche. We could produce many similar facts testifying to the extraordinary care and attention given to crèches in the Soviet Union. And every mother who leaves her child at a Soviet crèche can rest assured that it will receive care in no way inferior to that which it might receive at home—as thousands of letters of appreciation from parents testify.

The work of the crèche is arranged to accord with the working hours of the mother. Thus there are shift crèches which look after children only during working hours, and " prolonged " crèches, which take charge of them for ten or twelve hours a day. There is another type of crèche where children stay for twenty-four hours, or even permanently; in the latter case they go home on free days. There are also " periodic " crèches, which look after children when their mothers work on night shifts.

The most popular are the shift crèches; but " prolonged " crèches are also in great demand, particularly in industrial centres. Thus in 1933 " prolonged " crèches looked after 48·2 per cent of the total number of children served in Leningrad; in Ivanovo, the proportion was 53·5 per cent. We do not, however, consider it expedient to make this the chief type of crèche. Experience has shown that the shift crèche gives excellent results.

Notwithstanding the gigantic development of the crèche system in the Soviet Union, there are at the present time a large number of infants and young children not served by crèches. For them, the State has organised a widespread—one might almost say a universal—system of special medical consultation-clinics which keep young children under constant medical observation, and, when necessary, give them medical attention The " consultations " attend to all women who come to them for advice, preference being given to pregnant women and mothers; they organise group discussions, and lectures and exhibitions on the hygiene of pregnancy, child-bearing, and sex life; and on the care and feeding of infants. In the whole of the Russian Empire in 1914 there were altogether nine of these consultation-clinics; in the first year of the Soviet State this number was increased to 55; at the present time there are about 4,000 consultation-clinics in the Soviet Union. In 1934 they attended to 28,500,000 patients.

In his report to the Sixteenth All-Russian Congress of Soviets, the People's Commissar for Health, G. Kaminsky, described the work of the consultation-clinic in the Kalacheyev district of the Voronezh province: " This clinic has an enormous number of active women members. The meetings of the clinic dealing with problems of maternity and infant care attract hundreds of women. The clinic has become a real centre for training ranks of workers for the collective farm crèches. As a result, 90 per cent of all the children of crèche age in the district have been absorbed into the crèches."

The numerous children's " stations " and milk-kitchens are also of great importance in the care of the infant. In 1935, there were about 1,500 milk-kitchens providing food for those children that are not looked after in crèches. The diet is based on scientific principles which ensure the normal healthy development of the children.

LIFE FOR WOMEN

In addition to those public institutions that are open to all, we must also take note of a series of special institutions designed for special categories of mothers and children. First among them is the Home of Mother and Child, which provides a refuge during the month before childbirth and two or three months after it for women living under unfavourable housing conditions. This home provides ideally hygienic living-conditions for both mother and child during the most difficult period of their lives. In the whole of the Soviet Union in 1935 there were 391 homes of this kind, with 26,000 beds. In addition, there are Infant Homes, for the care of abandoned children, orphans, and children whose mothers are too ill to look after them.

Pre-school (infant) education is the second stage of communal education. It is designed for children from three to seven years, and has enormous significance in the education of the rising generation and in freeing women from household cares. The chief type of permanent institution for infant schooling in the Soviet Union is the kindergarten. Physical training plays an important part in its work, and abundant use is made of air, light, and water. The kindergartens inculcate habits of hygiene into the children and create the necessary foundation for producing a healthy rising generation.

Besides the permanent kindergartens, there are also seasonal ones—" summer kindergartens " in the open air. They are being widely developed in the Soviet Union, and their curriculum is based on the same principles as that of the ordinary kindergarten, except that particular attention is naturally paid to the children's physical development, to open-air games, and a fresh-air régime.

Infant education has to a certain extent been developed in all European countries (its feeble beginnings existed even in Tsarist Russia), but everywhere outside Soviet Russia it is left to the initiative of private individuals and charitable organisations. Only in the Soviet Union has infant education, like all other spheres of education, become the direct concern of the State.

Up to 1927–28, pre-school institutions served only a small number of the children in the towns, and still fewer in the country. Infant education began to develop in 1927–28, when the number of children in kindergartens increased from 86,500 to 308,400—that is, 3·5 times. (The number of pre-school institutions increased almost in the same proportion.)

During the period of the First Five-Year Plan and the first year of the Second the rate of growth of the kindergarten movement became progressively more each year.

Here is the increase in the number of children

in permanent and seasonal kindergartens throughout the Union:

	1927–28	1932–33	1935
Number of children in pre-school institutions (kindergartens and summer kindergartens) in thousands	308·4	5,291·2	5,858·8
(a) in towns	225·4	1,128·5	1,256·2
(b) in country	83·0	4,162·7	4,602·6

Thus the number of children in all types of kindergartens increased 19 times during the years 1928–35.

The proportion of children receiving infant education in the Union as a whole, in both town and country, in 1927–28 was 1·7 per cent of the total number of infants; in 1931–32 it was 12·6 per cent. In 1935, more than a quarter of the total number of children of pre-school age were attending kindergartens.

This progress is characteristic of the splendid achievements of the Soviet authorities in providing infant education for the children of workers; and it is all the more striking because, in essentials, the whole system had to be constructed from the very beginning, since infant education was practically non-existent in Tsarist Russia.

Particularly noteworthy are the successes achieved in developing infant education in the villages. Like the crèche system, the net of kindergartens in the villages spread very rapidly; and the number of children attending them increased 55 times as opposed to a sixfold increase in the towns. The chief form of kindergarten work in the villages lay in seasonal institutions—summer kindergartens. In 1935, more than half the children in the towns attended permanent kindergartens, which there developed more rapidly than the seasonal ones—though in the villages, too, the net of permanent kindergartens spread quickly during the First Five-Year Plan and recent years of the Second. The same reasons that produced such an exceptional rate of development in crèche services in the villages were responsible for the rapid growth of the kindergarten system. The intensive development of collective and state farms gave birth to forms of infant education and care for infants that were quite unknown in former times, and which enormously reduced the peasant woman's burden.

Children's institutions on the collective farms are particularly increasing because to a great extent they are created by the women workers themselves. It is no longer necessary to persuade women to leave their children in crèches and kindergartens. More and more frequently the woman worker on the collective farm, and often the individual woman peasant, is the prime mover in the organisation of kindergartens. They collect funds for food, choose people to manage the work, and so on.

In the Tartar republic, 90,000 children were served by crèches in the summer of 1934. Food funds were created for the crèches by women employed on the collective farms, and 2,690 of these women trained as managers and directors of crèches. The women of 2,251 collective farms in the Gorky district created a fund for summer crèches and kindergartens. In the Leningrad province more than 3,000 women workers on collective farms were trained and re-trained for crèche and kindergarten work. In 1934, in 15 districts of the Leningrad province, the women from the collective farms collected a food fund for the crèches which consisted of 5,590 centners of rye, 21 centners of oats, 2,940 centners of potatoes, and 1,121 centners of different vegetables.

In 42 districts of the Ivanov province, 2,500 of the best women from the collective farms were trained in courses of five or six months for work in children's institutions; and similar activities were in progress in the collective farms of the Crimea, Western Siberia, Sverdlovsk, Cheliabinsk, Moscow, and other provinces, districts, and republics. Many collective farms, indeed, gathered funds which made it possible to provide crèches and kindergartens for all the children on the farm.

These examples show that the crèches and kindergartens have become firmly rooted in the life of the collective farm. The workers, both men and women, realise the necessity for them, and, accordingly, have made them objects of their care. This is the first condition for the further extension and improvement of communal services for children, and it is also an essential step towards the further development of initiative and social consciousness among women in the villages. A letter written to Stalin in 1933 by the women collective farmers of the machine and tractor station of the Georgevsky district reflects this very clearly:

"And now, Comrade Stalin, we are planning how further to free the women collective farmers from bad living-conditions, how to lighten the burden of our lives in order to penetrate more deeply into public affairs and take a more active part in production. We already have crèches and kindergartens. During the spring and summer our children, from infants in arms to fourteen-year-olds, were taken care of in crèches and children's stations. The crèches for children at the breast were organised in the fields where the mothers worked. Now we are planning how to consolidate and improve this work. We must make our children's institutions models in every respect, so that the children will receive better care in them than at home. Collective farms should not begrudge funds for this work. Any money they spend will be amply repaid by more and better work from the women collective farmers."

The organisation of extra-school services for schoolchildren allows women to work, study, spend their leisure at the clubs, without having to worry about their children. This work with schoolchildren outside school hours is an important part of the general Soviet system of social education. The principal aim of extra-school work is to organise the leisure of the child and adolescent and fill it with occupations that will contribute to its health and happiness. Thus various kinds of technical and agricultural stations have been organised where children can satisfy their interest either in the mechanical arts or in agriculture. During the period of industrialisation, this interest increased among all classes of the population, including the younger generation. By the beginning of 1935 there were 625 of these stations in the R.S.F.S.R.

Other centres of extra-school work are the children's clubs (there were more than 300 of them in the R.S.F.S.R. in 1935), excursion bureaux, cinemas, theatres (more than 150 in the R.S.F.S.R.), different kinds of sports grounds, children's ski-ing stations and swimming-baths. In the summer, large numbers of schoolchildren spend their holidays at special holiday camps and sanatoria. Some idea of the extent of this work may be obtained from the fact that in 1934, 60,681 children were sent to summer camps from Moscow alone, 3,922 to sanatorium camps, and 13,876 to "Octobrist" camps (for children up to eight years of age). At the same time, children's playgrounds were organised in the squares, parks, and gardens of Moscow, and served as many as 20,000 children daily. In the parks, special groups of excursion leaders, entertainers, and physical-culture and art instructors were selected to serve as models for systematic work with children in all the other gardens, boulevards, and playgrounds of the capital.

We have already stated that in the Soviet Union crèche services and all forms of social education are organised by the State. The People's Commissariat of Health controls the crèche system and other services for infants. The People's Commissariat of Education is responsible for pre-school and extra-school work. All economic institutions help to finance these forms of social and educational work by setting aside for them, in accordance with the recent law of the Council of People's Commissariats of the

U.S.S.R. (July 1935), 0·25 per cent of all wages paid.

The trade unions also play a most important part in the organisation of social and communal services. " The trade unions should create conditions," said Shvernik, chairman of the All-Union Central Council of Trade Unions, " that will free the mind of the working woman from all worry while she is at work."

Trade unions exercise control over every aspect of the work of children's educational institutions by direct participation in the choice of administrative and teaching personnel. They also play an important part in financing this work. In the Soviet Union, the whole of social insurance is directly concentrated in the hands of the trade unions. The insurance funds, supplied by subscriptions from the employers of labour (and not by the workers), amount to a colossal sum of money (6,700,000,000 roubles in 1935). Out of this a large sum, which is constantly being increased, is allotted to services for children.

The expenditure of social insurance on services for children is given on the next page.

Thus we see that during the last five years the sums assigned by the trade unions to communal services for children have increased enormously—indeed, to 74 times the original amount. In 1935, these grants amounted to 438

TOWARDS A HEALTHIER

	In millions of roubles		
	1930	1932	1936
In all[1]	5·9	143·6	438·1
Crèches	2·2	76·2	181·0
Milk-kitchens	0·9	3·3	6·0
Infant homes	2·7	8·5	12·7
Summer health work (pioneer camps, sanatoria, etc.)	0·07	3·1	31·8
Kindergarten and other services for children	—	52·5	206·6

million roubles. In addition, quite considerable sums are allowed for this work in district governmental budgets. Thus in 1934, in the U.S.S.R., 201,600,000 roubles were allotted for the care of infants (as compared with 95,500,000 roubles in 1933), and 374,800,000 for kindergartens, infant homes, and extra-school work as compared with 239 million in 1933.

These sums, together with the wage percentage deducted in economic enterprises (which, taken in all, amounts to over 100,000,000 roubles), form the chief financial basis for the organisation of infant welfare and pre-school education. Parents pay only 25–35 per cent of the estimated expenditure: the rest is completely covered by funds supplied by the Government and the trade unions. This makes it possible not only considerably to extend the number of children served,

[1] Not including payments made to mothers for feeding children and infant layettes.

but also continually to improve the standard of educational work.

The growth of social forms of education among children and the widespread absorption of women into production do not in any way encroach upon the educational function of the mother. The policy of the Soviet authorities with regard to women does not belittle the educational functions of motherhood; on the contrary, it exalts them and creates the most favourable conditions for their full and fruitful realisation.

And in the task of looking after her children, participation in public life and work gives the woman opportunities of educating herself, raising her general cultural and political level, and acquiring definite pedagogical knowledge. This fully equips her for successfully educating her children. The mother fulfils her educational function chiefly inside the family; here both mother and child spend most of the time, and it is the family environment that, in conjunction with schools and other specialised forms of education, constitutes the chief factor in the formation of a child's character and in its spiritual and physical development.

On the other hand, women (and parents in general) take active part in the work of institutions of social education by giving them the most varied aid. In all Soviet schools there are assistance committees (" komsodi ") composed of parents of pupils and representatives of local public organisations. These committees help in the education of the children, particularly in the organisation of workrooms, study-rooms, and workshops. In the sphere of extra-school work, they organise, through the agency of the parents, the children's leisure, winter and summer playgrounds, etc. They also provide for hot lunches, dining-rooms, and school farms near the town (with vegetable gardens, sheep, goats, and poultry). In the schools there are, as well as the assistance committees, parents' groups for every class. These groups participate directly in the organisation of pedagogical work and in the work itself. They are composed chiefly of women—pupils' mothers who take an extremely active part in school organisation.

Widespread social work is being carried out in organising the family education of children. Mass conferences of parents are arranged, at which they compare notes with their children, discuss the work of the school, etc. Of late, problems of child education have been discussed everywhere— in the Press, in factories, in collective farms, in schools, in pupils' homes.

At the end of 1934 an extremely original and interesting competition was arranged among workers to decide on the best cultural education for children. Throughout the country, people are taking part in this competition.

In addition to communal education, the organisation of communal restaurants is of enormous importance in improving conditions of life for women. A woman's time-table in 1930, when communal restaurants and similar services for workers' families were still in their infancy, showed that a woman factory-worker spent an average of half the time she devoted to domestic work in cooking; the woman who did not go to work spent 47 per cent of her time in cooking.

The Soviet Union has great achievements to its credit in the organisation of communal food services. During the period of the First Five-Year Plan the figures for the towns were as follows:

	1928	1932
Number of workers fed by communal restaurants in the towns of U.S.S.R. (in thousands, at the end of the year)	750	14,800
Number of dishes produced every 24 hours by communal food services (in thousands, at the end of the year)	2,200	29,000

These figures show that from 1928 to 1932 the number of people served by communal restaurants in the towns increased 20 times, and the number of dishes about 14 times. In 1933, the number of people served by communal restaurants in the towns was 15,700, or 37·2 per cent of all the urban population.

Particularly outstanding were the achievements of the communal restaurants in the chief branches of national commerce and industry. According to figures of the State Planning Commission, the number of metal-workers served in communal restaurants increased from 16 per cent on January 1, 1928, to 75 per cent on January 1, 1933; in the building trade from 6·4 per cent to 74 per cent; among transport workers from 3·4 per cent to 68 per cent; among miners from 11·4 per cent to 72·5 per cent. In 1933, 75·5 per cent of the pupils in universities were provided with meals. In Moscow alone, two-thirds of the population, or 2,370,000 people, were being fed by communal restaurants by October 1, 1933. The number of people served by communal restaurants in the country (state farms, machine and tractor stations; the turf, timber, and fishing industries) was 2,450,000 in 1933.

Meals for children are organised on a gigantic scale. In 1933, 72 per cent of the total number of children in the schools were supplied with meals by communal restaurants. This work is particularly well developed in large towns and industrial centres. In Moscow, the number of children fed by communal restaurants increased from 128,000 in 1931 to 391,000 in 1933; the number of children's restaurants more than five times (320). The provision of free and semi-free meals for children was also greatly developed. By the end of 1933, about 60,000 children were in receipt of meals at reduced prices.

The quality of the food served in communal restaurants has been greatly improved during recent years. For example, the children's restaurant attached to school No. 12 in Moscow provides two-course hot lunches for 2,047 schoolchildren daily, three-course dinners for 1,221, free dinners and lunches for 652, and especially nourishing food for 150 ailing children. The restaurant has a laboratory attached to it, where all produce used in preparing meals is analysed.

The further development of communal restaurants (1934-35) may be gauged from the figures for the total financial turnover of the communal food services. For the whole of the Union, it was 7,430,000,000 roubles in 1934, as compared with 4,852,000,000 in 1932 and 350,000,000 in 1928. For nine months of 1935 it was 5,180,000,000. And as the communal restaurants become still more numerous the trivial and exhaustingly monotonous task of cooking for the family will become smaller year by year.

The whole food industry in the Soviet Union has also grown at a colossal rate. Not so long ago, many workers had to bake their own bread;

TOWARDS A HEALTHIER

to-day there are large bakeries in all the chief towns and industrial centres which supply excellent bread to the whole of the urban population. Collective bread-baking, organised at the initiative of the women themselves, is widely practised in the villages and on state and collective farms. Other branches of the food industry are also being rapidly developed—confectionery, canned goods, butter, fish, etc. Home-prepared food products are being more and more replaced by the produce of factories in which an excellent variety of nourishing foods can be produced.

A. Mikoyan, the People's Commissar for the Food Industry in the Soviet Union, said in a speech at the second session of the Central Executive Committee of U.S.S.R. in January 1936: " Can we make our women tractor-drivers, combine-drivers, women like Maria Demchenko, stay at home and bake bread ? Can we make them wear home-made clothes ? This is now out of the question." Indeed, the Soviet woman of to-day, whether she works in a factory or on a collective farm, has learnt the value of her time. She prefers to spend it, not in the kitchen, but in work, study, educating her children. Factory preparation of food products on the Soviet scale largely frees women from wasting time and labour in the kitchen.

The organisation of communal laundries is also

of great benefit to women, since it frees them from the drudgery of washing-days. Before the Revolution there were only 13 communal laundries in the towns; by 1935 there were 180—and, in addition, the scope of these laundries had been very much extended. It has been estimated that by 1937 there will be mechanised laundries capable of satisfying the needs of all the urban population of the R.S.F.S.R.

But even more remarkable is the existence of communal laundries in the villages, where formerly they were quite unknown. This is what the collective farmers of the machine and tractor station of the Georgevsky district, North Caucasus, wrote to Stalin in 1933:

"We are also planning communal laundries. This is quite a new thing for the country. But we are not afraid of novelties. A communal laundry should be organised in every collective farm or, better still, in every brigade. And it is not so very difficult. They say there are washing machines in which the linen is washed, wrung, and dried by electricity. Well, for the time being we'll get along without washing machines. We'll have them, of course, in the future; in the meantime, all we need is a pair of medium-sized boilers, some tubs, and some irons, and there's your collective farm laundry. . . . That's not so difficult to organise."

The creation of various kinds of dressmaking and repair shops is also of great practical help in lightening the burden of women's everyday responsibilities. Of late, many of these shops have been organised, chiefly in the towns.

These are all different aspects of communal services which play a decisive part in transforming the everyday life of the working woman. Freed from the cares of a household, she can now emerge on to the highroad of public work, public activity, and cultural development. Her rôle as educator of the rising generation is thereby elevated to a much higher level.

In addition, the emancipation of woman from numerous household cares plays an important part in the organisation of healthy conditions of life and work for women in general. Governmental and social institutions pay constant attention to the health of the working masses. G. Kaminsky, the People's Commissar of Health in the R.S.F.S.R., said in a speech at the Sixteenth All-Russian Congress of Soviets in 1935:

" In our health services the interests of the masses are paramount. We strive to prevent the workers and collective farmers from falling ill, but if they do they must be speedily and thoroughly cured. We strive that children may be born and grow up in good living-conditions; that they may develop well physically; that the people may have good and healthy children, better than themselves."

There is a whole body of measures directed towards this end which encompasses all aspects of the life and work of the people. Maternity and infant care play an enormous part in safeguarding women's health. We have already described the Soviet legislation in this sphere—particularly, prolonged leave for pregnancy and child-bearing (16 and 12 weeks) on full pay, intervals for feeding babies, and other special laws, which, in conjunction with the general labour laws (enforcing a seven-hour working day, annual holidays, etc.), fully guarantee the preservation of the working mother's health and her power to work. They also guarantee normal health to the child.

The extent of maternity aid in the Soviet Union may be judged from the following figures: in 1935, 203,000,000 roubles were paid to women workers and employees during pregnancy and child-bearing, as compared with 30,000,000 roubles in 1929. In addition, 82,000,000 roubles were spent on special grants in respect of child-bearing and the nursing of infants. This marked increase in maternity grants during recent years is due to an increase in the number of women employed in national commerce and industry as well as to a rise in the birth-rate in a number of towns and provinces in the Soviet Union.

The organisation of lying-in facilities is particularly important in safeguarding the health of mothers. In 1935 there were 42,800 beds in lying-in hospitals in the Soviet Union as compared with 6,800 in 1914. The towns are adequately equipped with these hospitals, many of which are model institutions.

The lying-in services in the villages are still insufficient; and at the present time they serve only 20 per cent of the mothers. But even this represents a colossal achievement when we remember that there were lying-in facilities for only 4 per cent of the rural population in 1913.

The further development of lying-in services in the country is one of the most important problems of public health. In many administrative districts much has been achieved in this respect. In the Moscow district the percentage of women provided with qualified medical aid in childbirth (in lying-in hospitals, hospitals, etc.), has risen to 30 per cent, in Karelia to 43 per cent.

But even these achievements do not satisfy the increased demands of women in the new collective farm villages. In practically every memorandum to the village soviet there is a clause put forward by the women of the collective farms: " We must open a lying-in home that is clean, warm, and well run; where our children will be born amidst comfortable surroundings and grow up in them from the cradle."

In response to the growing demands and urgent needs of these women a remarkable and unprecedented new movement has grown up in the Soviet countryside for the organisation of collective farm lying-in homes out of funds supplied by the farms themselves. District lying-in homes and hospitals, even if there were enough beds in them, could not serve all the women on collective farms, for purely territorial reasons. Frequently the district homes and the doctors in attendance are twenty, fifty, even a hundred kilometres from the collective farm. A lying-in hospital in the farm itself would bring aid to the very door of the women workers.

The movement for organising lying-in homes in the collective farms has spread far and wide, and it aims at increasing the number of beds in these homes to 9,000 during 1936. The Tartar republic has been particularly active in this respect. Until quite recently Tartar collective farms were almost practically devoid of lying-in services. To-day, the republic has 52 exceptionally well-equipped lying-in homes on collective farms. Lying-in homes are also being organised on an extensive scale in the Ukrainian republic, the birthplace of the movement.

Collective farms give up their best houses for

lying-in homes, and frequently build new ones for this purpose.

Organs of public health in the Soviet Union give considerable aid to the collective farms in the organisation of lying-in homes. The Government has authorised the payment from State funds of midwives in collective farm lying-in homes; it has also ordered the public health administration to provide these homes with trained medical staff. There can be no doubt that these measures will greatly facilitate the further growth and consolidation of this new enterprise.

General medical aid has been greatly developed by the Soviet State. The number of permanent hospital beds in all kinds of medical institutions (excluding sanatoria and institutions for the preventive treatment of disease) in Tsarist Russia was 175,600. In the Soviet Union, it had risen by 1928 to 246,100; by 1935 to 525,000. In 1935 the number of hospital beds in the Soviet Union was three times as great as in Tsarist Russia.

The funds assigned to public health services have also been enormously increased. In 1913, the rate of public health expenditure in Russia was 92·2 kopecks per head per year. In the Soviet Union in 1935 it was 30 roubles 59 kopecks. In all provinces and districts, in town and country, in large centres and provincial towns, the population is thoroughly aware of the improvements in the provision of medical aid and in the whole system of public health services.

In the Soviet Union, sanatoria, spa treatment, and rest homes have been organised on a gigantic scale. In Tsarist Russia, sanatoria and spas were the privilege of a very limited circle of wealthy people. To-day, they are within the reach of any worker; and it has become literally the recognised thing to go to a rest home during one's annual holiday. Wide use is also made of sanatorium and spa treatment. In 1935, 579,000 people were treated in spas and sanatoria and 1,613,000 visited the rest homes of the trade unions. The majority (about 70 per cent) of those receiving treatment or in rest homes are maintained free of charge at the expense of the social insurance funds; and 90 per cent of those thus maintained are workers or people belonging to the equivalent categories (engineers, technical and scientific workers). Women constitute 30 per cent of the people sent to rest homes, and there are also special rest homes for pregnant women and nursing mothers in which everything, from medical attention to diet and general routine, is designed to assist in every possible way the health of mother and child.

It is scarcely necessary to emphasise the enormous influence of the sanatoria and the spa services in improving the health of the workers. By inculcating the fundamental principles of hygiene into their patients they exercise an immediately beneficial influence on the everyday life of the masses. Workers take away from them not only the health and strength they have acquired during their stay, but also habits of personal hygiene and a healthy mode of life— a routine of living which considerably prolongs and consolidates the effects of the treatment they have received, and which produces further improvement in their health and physique. All these measures for improving general medical services, maternity aid, sanatorium, and spa treatment, are at the service of everybody without distinction of sex, and they contribute enormously towards a healthier environment for women.

One of the most important factors in safeguarding and improving the health of women workers in the Soviet Union is the legislative measures that are directed towards improving the actual conditions under which they do their work. In addition to the general legislation of this character, which we studied in the first chapter, much is being affected by the widespread application to industry of various rationalising measures which eliminate the danger of specific harm to women. Some fifteen scientific institutes, employing many research workers, take part in this work.

For example, women are employed without any harm to the female organism in many branches of heavy and ordinary machine construction. This is made possible chiefly by mechanising the movement of parts on to the lathe and automatically fixing them there.

Another kind of rationalisation which makes it possible to employ women in work of this kind without any structural adaptations of ordinary factory equipment is the isolation of processes demanding special physical effort— e.g. fixing and mounting machines. These difficult processes are reserved for a special group of workers and, when this has been done, the remaining operations can easily be performed by women.

In the most important branches of the chemical industry, the employment of female labour is made undesirable, since poisonous substances are present in the air which exercise a more harmful effect on women than on men. These poisons are particularly injurious to pregnant women, and may adversely affect both the birth and the survival of the child. The chief means of combating this danger in the Soviet Union is the mechanisation and sealing-off of the processes that give rise to injurious conditions; and the progress that has been made in this direction is clearly illustrated by figures supplied by the Leningrad Institute for the Organisation of Labour and the Protection of Workers' Health. According to these statistics, women were employed in only 10 of 39 processes carried on in the old factories manufacturing chlorine, caustic soda, and barium chloride, of the Bereznikov Chemical Combinat. In the new factories manufacturing syntheses of ammonia, nitrous acid, ammonium nitrate, and nitrate of sodium, which are supplied with better technical equipment, women are employed in 36 of the 41 processes.

The widespread improvements that have taken place in working conditions, such as artificial ventilation, improved water supplies, better industrial lighting, special working clothes, and adequate sanitation, have produced markedly happy results, especially among the women. Before the October Revolution there was one bath-house to every ten coal-shafts; by the end of the First Five-Year Plan there were nine bath-houses to every ten shafts; and the funds allotted for building these bath-houses are being increased yearly.

What are the actual effects of all the factors we have described in improving the conditions of work and life for Soviet women? The remarkable successes achieved by the Soviet State in the safeguarding and improvement of the workers' health, particularly that of the women, are most clearly illustrated by the death-rate statistics.

The death-rate in Tsarist Russia was exceptionally high. It was about 30 per thousand in the national republics in 1913 and even higher in the villages. By 1931 it had been lowered by almost a third.

After 1931, it continued to decline. In the Ukrainian Republic it was 12·8 per thousand in 1935, as compared with 21·2 in 1913; in the White Russian Republic, 13 as compared with 17·8 in 1913. This is an extremely rapid rate for a decline in the death-rate. In Western Europe, a similar decrease has taken place only over a period of more than half a century (1841–50, 26·6 per cent; 1901–1905, 19·9 per cent).

The decline in the death-rate in the Soviet Union is naturally accompanied by an increase in the expectation of life among workers. The average length of life for a woman in 1907–10 was 33·9 years; for a man, 31·9. In 1926 (the year of the last general census) it was 46·8 years for a woman and 41·9 for a man.

Maternity and infant care in the Soviet Union have produced a sharp decline in the death-rate for children. In 1909, the rate for children less than a year old was 29·52 per cent in the towns and 28·82 per cent in the country; in 1926, it was 17·21 per cent in the towns and 18·98 per cent in the country.

In Moscow we can trace the fall in infant mortality over a longer period. Between 1900 and 1904 the death-rate for children less than a year old was 34·6 per cent; this decreased to 27·9 per cent in 1914, then, during the war, increased to 35·5 per cent. After this, there was a steady decline to 23 per cent in 1920—lower than the pre-war level—and an even more rapid fall to 12·4 per cent in 1930. Infant mortality in Moscow under Tsarist rule was the highest among the large cities of the world. To-day the Soviet capital has one of the lowest infant mortality rates in the world.

Of great interest in this connection are statistics that show the general standard of health among the rising generation. In 1885 a mass examination of children was conducted in Glukhov (Moscow province) by the scholar Erisman; and similar surveys were made in 1927 and 1934 by the People's Commissariat of Health.

In 1885, the average height of a boy of $14\frac{1}{2}$ years was 141·2 cm. In 1934, that of a boy of 14 years (six months younger) was 146·2 cm.—5 cm. taller. In the first case the weight of the $14\frac{1}{2}$-year-old boy was 35·2 kilos; in the second, 37·4 kilos.

Chest measurement in the first case was 69·2 cm.; in the second, 71·8 cm.

Statistics showing the improvements in the physique of girls are even more striking. In 1885 the height of a 14½-year-old girl was 143·5 cm.; in 1934 that of a 14-year-old girl (six months younger) was 148·5 cm. The chest measurement of a 14½-year-old girl in 1885 was 71·1 cm.; in 1934 that of a 14-year-old girl was 73 cm. and that of a 15-year-old girl 75·4 cm.

No less significant are the statistics of illness among women workers. Figures published by the Central Administration of Social Insurance show that, as a result of increased material prosperity, the improvement of communal services, and the active enforcement of labour hygiene, illness among workers, particularly among women, has in recent years steadily declined.

In the course of four years (1930–34), illness among women workers in machine-building decreased by 25 per cent, and in the cotton industry by almost 20 per cent. In the overwhelming majority of other branches of industry the decline in the illness rate proceeded even more rapidly. In the coal-mining industry it fell by 34 per cent during the period 1930–33; in the glass industry by 35 per cent; in the rubber industry by 42 per cent; in the bootmaking and sewing trades by 45 per cent; in the confectionery industry by 44 per cent; in the match industry by 47 per cent, etc.

The number of cases of industrial poisoning is also decreasing rapidly in the Soviet Union. During the First Five-Year Plan, cases of chronic lead and aniline poisoning were cut down to a quarter of the former figure; benzine poisoning to a tenth; zinc oxide poisoning to a seventeenth.

Particularly characteristic of the Soviet Union is the fact that the illness rate is lower for women workers than for men—lower, for example, by 27 per cent in metallurgy in 1934, and by 6·5 per cent in machine-building. Moreover, the illness rate for women, between the ages of 20 and 27 —a period when, in other countries, illness is far more prevalent among women than among men —is less than that for men.

These favourable indices for women workers are extremely stable, both with reference to the chief groups of illnesses and to different kinds of work. One cannot, therefore, advance the theory that differences in the kind of work performed chiefly account for the discrepancy in the illness rate for men and women. It is particularly significant that in the case of nervous diseases, illness among women workers is—in contrast to the experience of capitalist countries—less frequent than among men. In general, too, the morbidity rate is declining more rapidly among women than among men.

These marked improvements in the health of women are due to the fact that in the Soviet Union the causes which formerly contributed to a higher morbidity rate among women have now been destroyed. A shorter working day and the development of communal services have considerably lessened the burden of woman's work and freed her from those cares which formerly oppressed her.

Besides improving all aspects of woman's life and work, and freeing her from household cares, we also strive to make the life of the woman worker more satisfying, more cultured. " The present-day worker is not what he once was," said Stalin at the Conference of Leaders of Industry on June 23, 1931. " The present-day worker, our Soviet worker, wants to live so that all his material and cultural needs are satisfied—his food supplies, his housing conditions, and his cultural and all other needs."[1] These words fully apply to the woman worker.

The present large-scale construction of dwelling-houses in the Soviet Union is of enormous importance in transforming the life of the worker. Under the First Five-Year Plan, the Government invested the colossal total of 4,000 million roubles

---

[1] Stalin, *Leninism*, vol. ii, " New Conditions—New Tasks," p. 376.

in house-building, and during the first three years of the Second Five-Year Plan (1933–35) over 5,000 million have been spent. During the First Five-Year Plan, 23,500,000 square metres of new living-space were provided. Housing facilities in the coal-mining industry increased by 2·5 times; in the ferrous metals industry by almost four times. During the three years of the Second Five-Year Plan, 20,500,000 square metres of new living-space have been constructed.

There has been a great improvement in the housing conditions of the workers. In the Don Basin, for example, all the workers who now live in spacious new apartments formerly lived in mud huts. Before the Revolution, 40 per cent of the workers in the Ukraine lived in mud huts.[1] To-day the mud hut has become a sort of historical monument. In Gorlovka, in the Don Basin, for example, a single mud hut is preserved as a reminder of how workers once lived.

During the period of the First Five-Year Plan, the construction of dwelling-houses was accompanied by a thorough reorganisation of municipal services. New towns were created. In place of the dirty, dusty roads so characteristic of the old Russia, proper paved roads were laid down, some of them asphalted. Towns are being planted

---

[1] State Planning Commission of the U.S.S.R.; *Results of the First Five-Year Plan*, Russ. ed., p. 186.

with gardens and provided with water-supplies, drainage, trams, and buses.

Under the First Five-Year Plan, 1,848,000,000 roubles were spent on public services (trams, drainage, water-supply, etc.)—three times more than in the preceding five years. So far, in the three years of the Second Five-Year Plan, 3,433,000,000 roubles have already been spent.

The standard of material well-being in a worker's family is rising sharply. The average monthly income of such a family has, according to figures of the State Planning Commission of the U.S.S.R., risen from 132·7 roubles in 1929 to 425·3 in 1935.

In 1935 and 1936, as a result of the Stakhanovite movement, the wages of men and women workers in the Soviet Union show a still further increase. At the same time the cost of food and other articles of wide consumption is being systematically lowered; and consequently the worker's standard of life rises in proportion.

Here is a characteristic example of the well-to-do life prevalent among workers' families in the Soviet Union: The Donetz District Administration of the People's Economics Statistics enquired into the living conditions of eighteen miners' families in its area. In 1933 these families were all living in barracks. Now ten families live in their own individual cottages, built with the aid of the State, and the other eight are living in a large new apartment house. All eighteen families have curtains and flowers in their rooms; the walls are hung with portraits and pictures. They also have wardrobes, nickel-plated bedsteads, chests, cupboards, bookshelves, radios.

The production of objects that create better living-conditions for the workers far exceeds that of other branches of production. In 1935, 285,000 gramophones, 7,250,000 records, and 324,000 bicycles were manufactured ; during 1936, 955,000 gramophones, 51,000,000 records, and 800,000 bicycles will be produced.

But even these advances are not enough to satisfy the growing demands of the masses. New conceptions of culture in everyday life are very clearly reflected in the general striving after order and cleanliness in the home and in personal hygiene. The watchwords of this struggle have taken deep root in the consciousness and habits of Soviet workers and peasants, and have penetrated to the furthermost corners of the Union; and the most active and outstanding workers in the cause are, as a rule, girls and women employed in factories and on collective farms, and the wives of workers and others in the home.

The workers on collective farms now endeavour to live in clean, well-ordered houses and to wear neat, clean, town-made clothes. In an address given at a conference of the Arzamas district to the girl workers on the collective farms of the whole of the Gorky district, some of the girls emphasised the necessity for reorganising their cultural life.

" Let us turn to the problem of our own living-conditions. We must admit that the inside of our huts is not all that could be desired. The windows are dirty, the atmosphere stuffy. Isn't it a disgrace that we should live in huts like these? Wouldn't it be far pleasanter for us to live in comfortable, clean rooms, with fresh air coming in, with curtains and flowers? We can easily attain this if only we are prepared to set about it. Let us not put it off until some future time. Let us organise a district competition for the best arranged, most comfortable collective farm hut. We girl farmers of the Arzamas district pledge ourselves to take part in this competition, and promise that by the spring sowing our huts will be absolutely clean and in good order, and that we will fulfil this socialist pledge."

The urge of the masses towards a cultured, healthy, and happy life is vividly reflected in the mighty physical culture movement which has swept through the ranks of Soviet workers. In Tsarist Russia, only a few wealthy young people devoted themselves to sport. In the Soviet Union, 8,200,000 people were enrolled in the physical culture movement by the beginning of 1935, and every year the number increases.

In 1935, the movement had 2,000,000 women adherents. In September of that year, women constituted 29 per cent of the total number of members of the trade unions' physical culture units.

The distribution of men and women throughout the different branches of sport in the summer season of 1935 was as follows:

THE DISTRIBUTION OF MEN AND WOMEN IN DIFFERENT BRANCHES OF SPORT IN PERCENTAGES OF THE TOTAL NUMBER OF PARTICIPANTS

	Gymnastics	Field sports	Swimming
Men	15·7	23·9	3·7
Women	27·7	34·3	5·3

	Volleyball	Tennis	Chess	Other sports
Men	12·5	1·3	16·4	27·5
Women	17·3	2·0	6·4	7·0

In general, men and women are more or less equally distributed throughout the various sports, though women are still very much in a minority among chess and draughts players, and are in a majority where gymnastics and field sports are concerned. It is interesting, also, to note that among workers belonging to agricultural trade unions the number of women in the physical culture movement almost equals that of men.

Soviet women have achieved great distinction in all forms of mass sport.

Among the 2,000,000 women in the physical culture movement there are tens and hundreds of thousands of outstanding swimmers, skiers, rowers, ice-skaters, etc. More than 350,000 women have passed the test for the Labour and Defence badge, which demands a high standard of skill in all the chief kinds of sport. Among these women there are many who are famous not only in the Union but throughout the world.

In the summer of 1935, the best performers in all kinds of sport competed in the all-Union physical culture "spartakiad" of the trade unions: among the entrants, 3,220 were men, 1,145 (35·6 per cent) women. Four world's records were established at this meeting, all of them by women.

World's records in women's athletics held by Soviet women are given on p. 188.

Ten of thousands of women take part in long-distance sports expeditions. In 1935, 2,120 women took part in climbing expeditions in the Caucasus and 265 of them reached the summits.

Five wives of Red Army commanders, Vaggina, Dyachenko, Irdugan, Ugolkova, and Ulitina

TOWARDS A HEALTHIER

WORLD'S SPORT RECORDS HELD BY SOVIET WOMEN

Sport	Record holder	Year	Result	Former record
300 metres	Buikova (Moscow)	1935	41·6 sec.	48·6 sec.
400 ,,	,,	1935	59·5 ,,	1 min. 0·4 sec.
500 ,,	,,	1935	1 min. 16·8 sec.	1 min. 17·3 sec.
Throwing the spear	Maslova (Leningrad)	1935	62·20 metres	57·05 metres
Skating 5,000 metres	Kuznetsova (Gorky)	1935	10 min. 21·2 sec.	10 min. 33·6 sec.
,, 500 ,,	,,	1936	48·2 sec.	49·1 sec.

188

covered, in the winter of 1935, the enormous distance of 3,000 kilometres from Tumen to Moscow on skis in one month twenty days (January 3 to February 23)—a feat demanding enormous endurance and thorough training.

We have examined all the different factors that are transforming the life of women in the Soviet Union by improving their health and raising their standards of culture. We have seen how large scale creation of communal services is combined with scrupulous attention to the needs of every individual worker and his family. We have endeavoured to show that the reorganisation of the workers' environment is closely bound up with the widespread attraction of women into public work and activity, and how this conjunction underlies the whole of the mighty socialist reconstruction of women's lives.

In conclusion, let us for a moment consider a problem of no little importance. In western Europe, the theory that industrial work is harmful and dangerous to woman and her offspring is still fairly widely held; and it is based on the abundant material to be found in capitalist countries, which shows the existence of a higher illness rate among women than among men. In the majority of countries, women become totally unfit for work earlier than men. Among women workers—particularly young women—

anæmia, nervous diseases, and other general organic ailments are more frequent than with the males.

Particularly noticeable is the incompatibility of work and child-bearing. Among women workers, there are a large number of miscarriages, premature births, and illnesses after child-bearing. Statistics also show that the mother's participation in hired work leads to an increase in infant mortality. From these facts the conclusion is drawn that woman's place is not in the factory, but in the home, looking after the family.

The material and statistics we have referred to in the course of this book wholly refute this theory. They show that with the active social policy of the Soviet State, directed towards making all aspects of work and life healthier, the employment of women and the safeguarding of their health and that of their children in no way exclude each other, but, on the contrary, are interdependent. Under Soviet conditions, women participate in rationally organised work, and at the same time display wider interests, a steady development in personality, and an improvement of health which is also evident in their families. Here, therefore, is no incompatibility. On the contrary, everything combines to hasten on the real and complete emancipation of women to which all Soviet policy in this sphere is unswervingly directed.

CHAPTER VII

CULTURAL GROWTH AND SOCIAL ACTIVITY AMONG WORKING WOMEN

THE DEVELOPMENT OF WOMEN as workers is closely connected with the development of their social and cultural standards; these considerations mutually condition and supplement each other. The Soviet State from the very beginning of its existence set itself the task of raising the cultural level of women and attracting them into public life, and forthwith began to accomplish this task. Liquidation of illiteracy on a mass scale was begun in 1919; and as early as 1920 women took a considerable part in electing deputies to the Soviets. But the most profound and decisive changes in the social and cultural level of women belong to the years of the First and Second Five-Year Plans.

Participation in national production has made possible the remarkable successes of Soviet women in the conquest of culture and in public life.

CULTURAL GROWTH

On the other hand, these successes greatly facilitated the consolidation and continuation of women's achievements in production. In the preceding chapters, we frequently emphasised the closeness of this tie between the development of women as workers, and their general social development. The most brilliant example of this interdependence is supplied by the Stakhanovite movement for the higher productivity of labour, which represents an enhanced degree of socialist public activity and clearly testifies to the new technical and cultural levels that have been attained by the men and women workers in the Soviet Union.

In this chapter, we shall investigate the general position regarding the social and cultural development of the women.

In Tsarist Russia, 70 per cent of the population was illiterate; among women workers and peasants the percentage was even higher. In 1920 the proportion was 67 per cent for the population as a whole and 77·5 per cent for the women.

The decree of the Council of People's Commissars for the liquidation of illiteracy which was issued on December 26, 1919, and signed by V. I. Lenin, marked the beginning of a determined attack on this widespread backwardness. As a result of systematic and persistent work, the percentage of illiterates was considerably lowered even during the period of the First Five-Year Plan. In 1929, at the beginning of this period, more than half the population (58 per cent) was literate. During the First Five-Year Plan the liquidation of illiteracy was speeded up, till in 1932 90 per cent of the population were already literate. This work is being continued under the Second Five-Year Plan with undiminishing intensity. On September 1, 1932, 9·2 out of every 100 working women were illiterate; by May 1, 1935, this percentage had been lowered to 6. Many tens of thousands of women workers who during this period had come from the villages and from homes to work in factories became literate.

The scope of this work in liquidating illiteracy and partial literacy may be gauged from the fact that within the four years during which the First Five-Year Plan was fulfilled, 45,000,000 people were taught to read and write. In 1935, there were 4,157,200 pupils of ages between 16 and 50 in schools for illiterates throughout the Union, and 5,375,500 in schools for partial literates and in the more advanced schools. More than half of these pupils were women. It is significant that the number of pupils in these schools is now beginning to decline in consequence of the marked decrease in the number of illiterates. Correspondingly, there is a noticeable increase in the number of pupils in schools for partial literates and in the more advanced schools which form the next step in adult education. According to the Plan for 1936, 3,000,000 people will be receiving instruction in schools for illiterates, and more than 7,000,000 in the more advanced schools which follow them.

Only an exceptional urge towards learning and knowledge among the toilers themselves, vividly expressed in the popular saying: " Learning is light, ignorance darkness," could have made possible the gigantic scale of this cultural and educational work, and the remarkable successes that have been achieved. This desire for knowledge was very well expressed by the women from the collective farms of the machine and tractor station of the Georgievsky district in their letter to Stalin:

" Of course, we must study much in order to be able to manage large farms properly. We want to study all the winter; to learn how to read and write; to study the fundamentals of political knowledge and scientific agriculture. Give us more books and note-books, because the desire to study is very great among the women. For example, Fekla Golovchenko, one of our active workers, almost fifty, gladly took to study. ' If I'm not properly educated,' she says, ' I can't handle my brigade.' They all say the same, young and old. Now that we are called upon to take part in the administration of public life and economy, education is no longer a luxury, it is an absolute necessity, like water for a thirsty man."

Together with this vast system of cultural and educational work among the adult inhabitants of the Soviet Union, obligatory schooling for the rising generation has been developed on a colossal scale in the primary and secondary schools. In 1914 there were 7,800,600 children in these schools; in 1928-29, the beginning of the First Five-Year Plan, there were 12,074,000; and in 1935-36, 25,569,100. During this period the number of girl pupils increased even more rapidly than the number of boys. In earlier years, a smaller number of girls entered the general schools than boys. In 1927-28, girls constituted only 39·6 per cent of the total number of pupils in these schools. At the present time this inequality in numbers has to a great extent (though not entirely) been overcome. In 1935-36, girls constituted 47 per cent of the total number of pupils. In the eastern national republics, the achievements in attracting girls into the schools were particularly creditable (cf. following chapter).

Nevertheless, the educational level of the young

CULTURAL GROWTH

women who have entered industry during the last few years has been somewhat lower than that of the men. An investigation of young workers conducted in January 1936 showed that among young women workers (up to twenty-five years of age) the percentage of those who had not completed primary schooling was twice as large as the corresponding percentage for young men. More recent achievements in drawing children into the schools are not yet being fully reflected in the educational level of the young people who are pouring into industry at the present time.

We showed in an early chapter that a large number of students in high and middle training schools were women (38 per cent among university pupils in 1935, and 44·1 per cent among students in the technical colleges). It is clear that the marked success of women in specialised training schools presupposes a higher standard of general education. Besides the middle school and Rabfaks (which are attached to universities and prepare students for them) there are many general and pre-university courses which are widely attended by women.

One of the chief forms of mass cultural and creative work in the Soviet Union is the clubs, which contribute in different ways to the workers' cultural development. Clubs and similar institutions in the Soviet Union increased from

27,700 in 1928–29 to 58,000 in 1935. The majority of these institutions are reading-rooms—the chief centres for extra-school work among the rural population. There were 33,900 of these rooms in 1935. The most extensive and profitable work is carried on in socialist culture centres, trade union and collective farm clubs. One of the most important kinds of work in clubs is based on creative self-expression of the workers—that is to say, work in various kinds of circles or groups. Circles are organised for the study of different arts and sciences, and for the encouragement of technical and practical activities. They are sometimes organised, not only in clubs, but also in the factories and industrial concerns themselves. At the present time they have an enormous number of members; and the development of these circles is, in fact, a most revealing indication of the cultural initiative and social activity of the masses. Therefore statistics showing the participation of women in these circles are of special interest.

Statistics collected by the All-Union Central Council of Trades Unions, as for April 1, 1933, show that the creative activity of women workers in circles of all kinds organised in factories and other industrial concerns is almost equal to that of the men; and the proportion of women among members of these circles is not much less than the proportion of women among workers in general. Thus, in all the circles investigated (97,000, with a membership of 2,179,000), the percentage of women was 25·9, and among workers in the factories to which the circles belonged, 33·7. In the industrial trade unions the corresponding figures are 27·7 per cent for women among members of circles, and 33 per cent for women among workers in general. Similar figures were obtained in other departments—State commerce, communal food services, social, cultural, and administrative institutions.

Women take an active part in newspaper work as worker or collective farm correspondents for various types of newspapers. According to the figures of the Central Administration of National Economy Statistics of the U.S.S.R., which cover 3,850 newspapers of different kinds—central, district, factory, state and collective farm—women constituted 12·7 per cent of the total number of contributors to these newspapers in 1933. Among contributors to factory newspapers (worker correspondents) women constituted 18 per cent.

It is interesting to note that about the same percentage of women write for the collective farm newspapers—17·4 per cent of the total number of contributors in 1933. We see, however, that the percentage of women among contributors to all types of newspapers is still less than the percentage of women in the general body of workers. But this does not in any way invalidate the significance of these figures as indications of the remarkable cultural development of women workers. The Soviet woman has not only become literate; she has, by contributing to the newspapers, already learnt how to use her literacy as a keen weapon in the struggle against numerous shortcomings in the economic construction and organisation of everyday life, and as an aid in the fulfilment of those urgent tasks which socialist construction puts before her in every branch of her work.

An investigation conducted among young workers in January 1936 produced interesting data respecting the cultural development of Soviet women. It shows that nowadays Soviet girl workers frequently visit the theatre and cinema, go to concerts, museums, and on excursions. For every woman worker under investigation there was a monthly average of 3·75 visits to entertainments, lectures, etc. In Tsarist times, the woman worker went to the theatre or cinema only in the most exceptional instances. Soviet girls go to cinemas, theatres, and concerts nearly as frequently as young men.

Literature has become one of the necessities of life to Soviet women, and the best Russian

CULTURAL GROWTH

literature is read by the majority of young women workers. Thus, 66 per cent of those investigated in machine-building, had read Pushkin's *Eugene Onegin*, 66 per cent Gorky's *Mother*, 51 per cent Gogol's *Dead Souls*, 48 per cent Tolstoy's *Anna Karenina*, 55 per cent Sholokhov's *Virgin Soil Upturned*. Stalin's speech at the Seventeenth Party Congress was read and studied by 67 per cent. Before the Revolution the woman worker had no access to literature, the classics were entirely foreign to her; more than half the total number of women workers were illiterate.

Exceptionally striking is the change in the cultural level of women employed on collective farms. Active participation in the life of the farm has very much widened the intellectual horizon of women in our Soviet villages. The interests of the peasant woman in former times did not extend beyond her family—at the most, beyond her own village. Collectivisation has brought it about that all the problems of socialist construction, so near to the heart of our people, as a whole, are made intelligible and vital for these women too. Formerly peasant women never read newspapers; indeed it was only very rarely that a newspaper was ever seen in the village. According to an investigation conducted in 1934, 28 per cent of all women on the collective farms between sixteen and twenty-four years of age regularly read the newspapers. Among older women the percentage is of course less; but, even among them, regular newspaper readers are by no means rare. The present-day woman on the collective farm passionately desires knowledge and the opportunity to study. In 1923, the individual peasant woman between thirteen and fifty-nine years of age spent an average of 9·7 hours per year on study and self-education. In 1934, the woman on the collective farm spent an average of 259·5 hours—two hours more than the male farm worker.

The improved standard of living and cultural level of the woman on the collective farm have considerably changed the manner in which village women spend their leisure. In 1934 a large number of women (32 per cent in winter, 22 per cent in summer) employed on the collective farms visited cinemas and theatrical performances. Among young women up to twenty-five years of age, more than half attend various entertainments of this kind. About a third of the young women on collective farms attend clubs and reading-rooms regularly throughout the winter. Formerly peasant women had no time for cultural pursuits, and the existence of clubs, cinemas, or a stage in the villages was very rare indeed.

At the present time the former chasm between town and country has disappeared. Year by year the general cultural level of the two, and the nature of the diversions enjoyed by women collective farmers and by women workers in the towns, become more and more similar. The raising of the Soviet woman's cultural level is indissolubly bound up with the growth of her political consciousness and social activity.

The chief form of creative social self-expression among workers in the Soviet Union is participation in socialist competition and shock-work. We are already acquainted with the concrete results which have been achieved in the sphere of production. All social activity in the Soviet Union is organised on the principles of socialist competition. By participating in it the worker voluntarily assumes certain obligations the fulfilment of which is considered to be a point of honour. These obligations usually take the form of definite tasks in production (the fulfilment or over-fulfilment of the plan, lowering of production costs, the lowering of defect percentage); but definite social work is also included. Therefore the best shock-workers and Stakhanovites in production are usually also the most active social workers.

Social activity has been intensively developed in the Soviet Union, and takes many different forms. Its chief mass expression, which incorporates both workers and employees, is the trade union. At the beginning of 1935, the trade unions had 19,319,700 members, of which 6,701,900 were women. Women constitute 34·7 per cent of the total number of trade union members, whereas for all workers (both members and non-members of trade unions) the proportion is 33·4 per cent. This shows that women workers have been drawn into the trade unions to a slightly greater extent than men.

Women take an active part in organising the work of these unions. In 1928, the number of women among the members of the local trade union committees in all trade unions amounted only to 18·8 per cent—a very much smaller proportion than the proportion of women in the general body of workers. In 1935, women constituted 26·1 per cent of all recorded members of local committees. Here we must note that in 1935 a whole series of trade unions, with a high percentage of women members, were left unrecorded. In them, naturally, the presence of women in the elected organs of the trade unions was greater than the average figures we have given. In the sewing industry, for example, women constituted 60 per cent of the members of local trade union committees; in knitwear, 63 per cent; in cotton, 45 per cent; and so on.

Even more striking are the achievements of women on responsible posts in the higher and middle links of trade union organisation. Thus, in 1928, women constituted 7·6 per cent of the workers in district trade union committees, and in 1935, 20·1 per cent. In the ranks of the central committees of the trade unions they constituted 11·6 per cent in 1928, and 17·9 per cent in 1935.

It is particularly important to note the prominent part played by women in the leading organs of the trade union movement. More than one-fifth of the members of " plenums " of the central and district committees of the trade unions are women who have been promoted to active trade union work. There are even quite a number of women at the head of trade unions in the Soviet Union. At the beginning of 1935, there were nineteen women chairmen and twelve women secretaries in the central committees of the trade unions. (The total number of central committees is 159.)

Moreover, the wives of specialists not engaged in work themselves have been widely drawn into social activity. This movement among engineers' wives arose in 1934, when the first group of women was organised by E. M. Vesnik during the construction of the Krivoi Rog Metallurgical Plant. Now many thousands of engineers' and other specialists' wives, in the most diverse factories, on construction sites, in widely separated districts of the Union, take an active part in the life of industrial concerns. On their own initiative they have assumed responsibility for various types of cultural and communal services—e.g. communal restaurants, crèches, kindergartens, the improvement of housing conditions. At the Dzerzhinsky Metallurgical Factory in the Ukraine, 450 out of 1,500 wives of engineers and technicians are now members of this " social detachment " of engineers' wives which only last year consisted of a handful of women.

The movement has developed on a similar scale in other large factories, and has achieved much in bringing order into cultural and communal services for factory workers, particularly on construction sites and in the new factories that have recently been erected in sparsely populated districts. At the Dzerzhinsky factory, these women have brought perfect order into ten workers' barracks; they have organised a kindergarten, a house for engineers and technicians, and a music studio, and have arranged sports and excursions. At the Ilyich factory in Kharkov, 45 wives of specialists joined in the organisation of technical study circles for workers and of a theatre for children. At the same time these specialists' wives themselves take courses, study industrial processes, join political debating circles, and study foreign languages.

This participation of specialists' wives in social

work has grown into a mighty movement, and has already produced its own leaders, such as E. M. Vesnik (Krivorozhstroi), M. C. Manayenkova (Dzerzhinsky factory), and S. I. Stein (Red Profintern factory). The organisation of the work takes definite practical forms. In all industrial centres there are conferences of specialists' wives at which they exchange experiences. In May 1936, an all-Union conference was called at which the Party leaders and members of the Government were present. This conference showed that the movement had trained a large number of women, who had till then been outside any active creative work, for participation in social activity and in socialist construction. Formerly these women had devoted themselves entirely to work in the home without deriving any satisfaction from it. The conference also gave prominence to the splendid work done by engineers' wives in different activities connected with industrial enterprises, particularly in improving cultural and communal services for workers.

On May 13, 1936, the Central Executive Committee of the U.S.S.R. awarded nine women, the initiators and leaders of the movement, with E. M. Vesnik, M. S. Manayenkova, and K. T. Surovtseva at their head, the Order of the Red Labour Banner; and thirty-one were given the

Order of the Sign of Honour. These awards were made for initiative shown by the wives of engineers and technicians in the organisation of the movement for better cultural and communal services for workers; and for energy shown in the development of the movement.

The growing social activity of women in the villages is chiefly reflected in their active participation in the organisation of the collective farms, and in the widespread promotion of women to administrative posts. In Chapter IV we described the splendid victories of women in this sphere. Here we need merely add that the social activity of women on the collective farms is not limited to their own farms.

District meetings and conferences of collective farmers, both men and women, are quite usual in the Soviet Union. The woman on the collective farm takes an active and important part in discussing the fundamental problems of collective farm organisation at the periodic all-Union conferences of collective farm shock-workers. Two hundred and twenty-four women were present at the first conference of collective farm workers in 1933, constituting 14·8 per cent of the total number of delegates. At the second conference (held at the beginning of 1935) there were 442 women delegates—almost a third (30·8 per cent) of the total number. With profound attention and complete understanding they discussed such an important problem as the new statute of the agricultural artel, and suggested a number of amendments and additions.

At the all-Union conferences of the best workers in grain-farming, the beet-fields, cotton-growing, live-stock raising, and flax-growing held at the end of 1935 and the beginning of 1936 with the leaders of the Party and members of the Government, at which the results of the agricultural year of 1935 were summed up, women played an important part. At some of the meetings (meetings of " five-hundreders " of the beet-fields and flax-growers) they were in a majority.

The co-operative store is an important factor in the economic life of the Soviet village. It is chiefly responsible for supplying the village with goods manufactured in the town. Women have taken firm root in the administration of these stores, and more than 100,000 of them work as members of managing bodies and on control committees of consumers' co-operatives.

The most important manifestation of the growing social activity of women in the Soviet Union is their participation in the work of the soviets. The number of men and women voters has increased almost threefold during the last six years; and the growth of women's participation in the election of deputies to the soviets is shown by the following figures for the number of women who vote at elections (in percentages of the total number of women with the right to vote):

Year	In towns	In villages
1926	42·9	28·0
1927	49·8	31·1
1929	65·2	48·6
1931	76·0	63·4
1934	89·7	80·3

At the elections of 1926, both in town and country, fewer women than men voted (the percentage of men who voted in the towns was 60 of the total number with the right to vote; the corresponding figure for women was 42·9 per cent; in the country, 68·5 per cent of the men voted and only 28 per cent of the women). In 1934, the percentage of women who voted was as great as that of men. Particularly high was the percentage of women members of the trade unions who voted in that year: it was 93, which equalled the percentage for male voters who were members of the trade unions.

V. Molotov, Chairman of the Council of People's Commissars, speaking at the Seventh Congress of Soviets on the proposed changes in the Soviet constitution, appraised the part played by women in the election of deputies to the soviets in these terms:

" It is impossible not to note the significance

of the growing participation of women in the elections to the soviets, which is the most important manifestation of the existence of a new many-millioned force which has been incorporated into the whole of socialist construction."

The limited number of female votes recorded in previous years may be partly explained by the fact that many women were either kept at home by domestic duties or had no one to look after their children, as also the noticeable increase in the number of women who now vote reflects the growing emancipation of women from the fetters of the home. But what these statistics chiefly show is the development of social and political consciousness, and the growth of social culture among Soviet women. During the years of Soviet power women have shaken off the confining influence of a closed circle of family cares and interests.

The increased social activity of women, with the growth of their participation in election campaigns, have further increased the part played by them in the work of the soviets, and the number of women in the soviets themselves.

Here are the comparative figures for the number of women elected to the soviets in different years.

	In thousands		
	1926	*1931*	*1934*
City soviets	18·7	43·0	50·2
Village soviets	122·6	317·0	329·6

AND SOCIAL ACTIVITY

	In percentage to the general number of deputies		
	1926	1931	1934
City soviets	18·0	25·9	32·1
Village soviets	9·9	21·0	26·3

In 1934, there were 380,000 women members of Soviets (in town and country districts) constituting 30 per cent of the total number of deputies. Particularly noticeable was the growth in the number of women (both in absolute and relative figures) in the village soviets; and the proportion of women among chairmen of village soviets also increased. In 1926, the percentage of women among chairmen of village soviets was only 0·6; and in 1927, 1·1 per cent. By 1931 it had risen to 5 per cent, and by 1934 to 7·7 per cent. In 1934, 16 per cent of the members of control committees in the village soviets were women (as compared with 14·2 per cent in 1931). In addition, there are more than 400,000 women workers in deputies' groups and sections of the soviets. Women are now also to be found in the People's Courts. In 1932 there were 20,000 women lay judges (32 per cent of the total number) in the towns; in the country there were 93,000—31 per cent of the total number.

In proportion to the growing participation of women in the lower ranks of workers in the soviets grow also their rôle and place in the supreme organ of soviet power, the All-Union Congress of Soviets. At the first All-Union Congress of Soviets there were 49 women——2·9 per cent of the total number of deputies; at the seventh congress, in 1935, there were 378 women—19 per cent of the total number of deputies. These figures illustrate the increasing part played by women in the political life of the Soviet Union.

A decisive part in the social and political life of the country is played by the Communist Party of the Soviet Union, which included in its ranks the vanguard of the working class, the most class-conscious, active toilers, devoted to the cause of socialist construction. A very important indication of the growth of social activity among Soviet working women is the steady absolute and relative growth of women in the Party. According to the figures of the central statistics department of the Communist Party of the Soviet Union, the percentage of women in the Party on January 1, 1928, was 12·8 per cent of the total number of Party members; on March 1, 1930, 14·7 per cent; and on October 1, 1933, 16·5 per cent.

While the general membership grows steadily, the rate of growth of the number of women Party members exceeds that of the general growth. From January 1, 1928, to November 1, 1933, the total number of Party members increased 2·1 times; the number of women in the Party almost 2·8 times. As to the social composition of the women Party members, one notes a continuous growth of the percentage of women workers and peasants. On January 1, 1928, 53·1 per cent of the women members of the Party were workers—12·7 per cent peasants, 34·2 per cent employees, etc. On January 1, 1933, 62·9 per cent were workers, 25·5 per cent peasants, and only 11·6 per cent employees, etc.

Among members of the Komsomol, the non-Party youth organisation, the rate of growth in the number of women is even more rapid than in the Party. On January 1, 1928, girls constituted 22·4 per cent of the total number of Komsomols (on January 1, 1925, only 15·7 per cent). By the middle of 1933—July 1—the percentage of girls had risen to 31·7—almost a third of the total number of Komsomols and about the same proportion as that of women in the general body of workers in the Soviet Union.

In the previous chapters we gave statistics, and many examples, of the promotion of women to leading administrative posts in factories, institutions, and in agriculture. With their new-found social development, the liberated and emancipated women take their place in socialist production side by side with the men, and are rapidly overcoming the cultural, social, and political backwardness they inherited from the past. Such is the triumph of Soviet policy in the sphere of female labour.

" Women represent half the population of the country; they represent an enormous army of labour, and their mission is to bring up our children, our future generation—that is to say, our future. That is why we must not permit this huge army of toilers to remain in darkness and ignorance. That is why we must welcome the growing social activity of our toiling women and their promotion to leading posts as an undoubted indication of the growth of our culture."[1]

But the Soviet woman participates actively not only in peace-time construction, both economic and cultural; she also takes an energetic part in the organisation of the defence of her fatherland. In the pre-revolutionary period, working women took part in the struggle of the workers; and in the days of the great October Revolution, which laid the foundation of the Soviet State, they actively fought in the ranks of the proletariat.

After the establishment of Soviet power the

[1] Stalin, Report to the Seventeenth Party Congress in *Socialism Victorious*, p. 53.

AND SOCIAL ACTIVITY

workers and peasants were not immediately allowed fully to transfer their revolutionary energy to peace-time construction. From 1918 to 1921, the Union was put to the bitter test of civil war. All the forces of the people had to be harnessed in order to conquer enemies millions strong. During this period women workers and peasants showed themselves worthy of the stern task of defending the Revolution. Women worked untiringly in the rear of the army; they carried on revolutionary work in the territory occupied by the enemy; they fought in the ranks of the Red Army as soldiers, scouts, machine-gunners, tank-drivers. Many women were awarded the Order of the Red Banner for exceptional heroism during the civil war.

The names of M. A. Solovyeva, a worker in the "Red Perekop" factory, who in 1917 took part in the formation of the Red Guards, and in 1918 fought in the ranks of the famous Chapayev division; of E. I. Nelsina, an old worker of the Urals, one of the first to enter the ranks of fighters for the Soviet State, first as a nurse, then on an armoured car; of the former agricultural labourer Anyshenok-Seglin, who in 1917 stormed the Winter Palace in the ranks of the workers—these names and many other are famous throughout the Union. In 1929, when the situation on the Far Eastern frontier became tense, many women volunteered for service in the Far Eastern Red Army. Raisa Rizhik fought shoulder to shoulder with the Red Army men, inspiring them by her example, for which she was decorated with the Order of the Red Banner by the Soviet Government.

By these examples Soviet women have shown in actual practice that, while they are heart and soul for peace, they are nevertheless prepared to fight for the independence and honour of their fatherland. This sentiment was expressed for the whole of the Union by the women workers of Leningrad in a letter to Stalin:

" We do not want war; we are occupied with creative work. But if we are attacked, all the worse for our enemies. All the workers, men and women, will consider it their sacred duty to defend the frontiers of the Union. We are prepared for war. The women workers of Leningrad will be in the front ranks, as they always have been. Women workers will go to the front; they will also take the place of their husbands, brothers, and comrades in the factories."

At the present time women workers and collective farmers are being more widely drawn into strengthening the defences of their country. On May 1, 1935, of the 12,733,000 members of the Osoaviakhim (Society for the Chemical Defence of the Soviet Union), 2,330,200, or

AND SOCIAL ACTIVITY

18·3 per cent, were women. There are Osoaviakhim circles in all the factories and on the collective farms. In them women acquire a knowledge of the technique of modern warfare, and learn the principles of anti-aircraft chemical defence.

In Osoaviakhim circles and camps, women learn how to use gas-masks and special gas-proof blankets and pass the P.V.C.O. tests (anti-aircraft chemical defence). As a practical measure, they create in every large house self-defence groups capable of minimising the consequences of an attack from the air. Without exaggeration, it may be safely stated that in the Soviet Union women have taken the leading part in mastering the principles of anti-aircraft and anti-chemical defence.

Soviet women are also prominent in all forms of mass-aviation sport. In the aero-clubs of the Osoaviakhim, girl Komsomols study aviation after working hours side by side with the men, and become excellent pilots.

Three or four years ago women pilots were exceedingly rare in the Soviet Union. In 1930, there was only one woman flyer, Z. Kokorina. During recent years hundreds of women flyers have been trained, and now hold an important place in sporting and civil aviation. Seven girls took an aviation course while working on the construction of the Moscow Metro. In 1935 they qualified for their pilots' licences. Three Tjurk women flyers, Kozieva, Askerova, and Agamirova, have graduated from the Baku Aero Club.

The Komsomolka O. Jordania, formerly a fitter at the Rion Hydro-Electric Station, now pilot in the Tiflis Aero Club, was awarded the Order of the Red Star in 1936 for outstanding achievements in aviation; and many Soviet girls have not only learnt how to fly, but have also established world's records.

Numerous women have taken up parachute jumping. Nina Kamneva, the most prominent of them and a holder of the Order of Lenin, established a world's record by a jump of 3,000 metres without opening her parachute for 2,700 metres. Her example was soon followed by other women. In March 1935, Vera Fedorova, also decorated by the Government, established the women's world record for an altitude jump of 6,350 metres without an oxygen supply. On June 17, 1935, six women parachute jumpers established a new world's record for an altitude jump without oxygen of 7,035 metres. Three of them, O. Yakovleva, A. Nikolayeva, N. Babushkina, all having had many excellent parachute jumps to their credit and having established this record, were awarded the Order of the Red Star; the other three, M. Bartseva, M. Malinovskaya, C. Blokhina, less experienced parachute jumpers, received Certificates of Merit of the Central Executive Committee of the Soviet Union.

On June 30, 1935, the Komsomolka Tamara Kutalova established a new record by jumping from a height of 7,750 metres. But even these records did not satisfy our women jumpers. On August 2, 1935, Anna Shishmareva and Galya Pyasetskaya established a new world's record for either sex by an altitude jump of 7,923 metres without oxygen. Both were awarded the Order of the Red Star.

Thousands of women have taken up gliding, and more than 2,000 of them have already passed the military technical gliding tests. Many work as staff and part-time instructors. In the autumn of 1935, a whole aerial train, consisting of an aeroplane and three gliders, travelled the record distance of 1,950 kilometres from Koktebel to Leningrad. All the pilots were women. On October 3, 1935, the glider Zelenkova established a world's record for sustained flight in a two-seater glider—12 hours 0·9 minutes. On the same day, Radenskaya set up a world's record for sustained flight in a single-seater glider—15 hours 39 minutes.

Shooting, with a view to obtaining the title of "Voroshilov Sharp-shooter," has been widely developed throughout the Union: 450,000 women

CULTURAL GROWTH

are learning to shoot and 100,000 of them have become Voroshilov sharp-shooters; 132 have earned the honourable title of "Master-shots."

Shooting competitions for women have been held in a number of districts and republics. Sixteen divisions—96 women in all—took part in the first competition which was held at the Minsk garrison in 1934. The best results were obtained by a division of women from the district military school, which scored 139 points out of a possible 150. But the best shooting by women was witnessed at a competition held with American marksmen. On this occasion, E. P. Senturina and Miroshnichenko, shooting from the "lying" position at a range of fifty metres, scored 100 points out of a possible 100. In the same competition, E. P. Senturina, the best shot in the Union, established a new record by scoring 396 points out of a possible 400. In recent years Senturina has established five all-Union records. Second place at the all-Union competition in the autumn of 1935 was taken by the Komsomolka N. Baranova, who also showed considerable skill.

Women are serving successfully in the ranks of the Red Army as junior, middle, and senior commanding staff officers. In 1935, there were 91 women in the ranks of middle and senior commanding staff officers, and 58 among junior staff officers. In the political and administrative economic sectors there were 637 women among middle and senior commanding officers, 418 among junior officers, and 24 among privates.

In military academies, schools, and training courses there are hundreds of women students—future commanders, pilots, air-mechanics. In 1935 there were 25 women students in the Zhukovsky Aviation Academy. In the Military Academy of Mechanisation and Motorisation there were 90—45 of whom were middle-ranking staff officers. In the Military Engineering Academy there were 41 women, and in the Military Engineering Academy of Communications 184.

Trained nursing has become popular among the inhabitants of the Soviet Union, particularly among the women. Red Cross and Red Half-Moon units have been created in factories and on collective and soviet farms during the last two years, and special first-aid courses and circles have been organised for training nurses. During the years 1929–32, the Central Committee of the Red Cross trained 342,087 people, the overwhelming majority of them being women. At these courses and in the Red Cross units, women receive, not only training in military nursing, but also instruction which enables them to introduce cleanliness and hygiene into the everyday life of workers in town and country.

This is characteristic of all our defence training, particularly that of women.

Work in the Osoaviakhim is one of the most striking and significant indications of the growth of social and political consciousness and activity among women; but even defence preparations are closely bound up with economic and cultural construction. The instruction in military nursing that is imparted to the population is indissolubly bound up with general education in health; it thus becomes part of the struggle for the introduction of culture and hygiene into everyday life. How closely these problems of defence and everyday hygiene are united in the work of the Red Cross nuclei can best be shown by concrete examples of the work of individual units.

S. Gavrilova, the best Red Cross organiser in the Chuvash Autonomous Province and head of a medical post on a collective farm, thus describes her work:

" Our medical post sees that cleanliness is observed everywhere. We insisted that there should be boiled water in the collective farm restaurant, that the floor should be clean and well scrubbed, and the dishes well washed. We wrote about the bad cooking in the wall newspaper and forced them to get a new cook. The medical post strives to bring order and cleanliness into every home. We make a note of the

AND SOCIAL ACTIVITY

dirty ones and tell the people how to keep them clean. Sometimes we organise voluntary help and help clean up the cattle-yards and put the huts in order. Such example serves for all the other collective farmers."

The chemical detachment of the Kalinin beet-producing collective farm led by Jdanovich has done extremely valuable work in destroying field pests.

These are varied manifestations of the growing cultural and social-political activity and initiative among women workers in the U.S.S.R. They affect all branches of social and cultural construction, as well as the defence preparations which are being organised throughout the country. The very diversity of these manifestations and their extraordinarily widespread mass character indisputably testify to the fact that Soviet woman has grown into a mighty social and cultural force.

CHAPTER VIII

WOMEN IN THE NATIONAL REPUBLICS

THE POPULATION OF THE U.S.S.R. is composed of many peoples. One hundred and ninety nationalities inhabit the territory of the Soviet Union; they form a brotherhood based on the principles of complete equality for all.

The Soviet policy directed towards achieving the complete emancipation of women is unswervingly put into practice in all the territories of the Union and among all the nationalities inhabiting them. The forms and methods of carrying out this policy, however, are not everywhere the same. In a number of national republics, there were tremendous difficulties to overcome—difficulties resulting from the peculiar historical position of women in these areas. To overcome these difficulties, special care and a special method of approach were required.

In Tsarist Russia, all so-called " small " nationalities were restricted and oppressed in every way.

NATIONAL REPUBLICS

The provinces and districts inhabited by these peoples had the status of colonies, and their poorer inhabitants were under the yoke of a twofold exploitation—by their own bourgeoisie, landowners, and priests, and by the Russian bourgeoisie. Thus these conquered peoples were doomed to stagnation and ruin, and in many cases to complete extinction. As a result, the majority of them remained at a very low level of economic, cultural, and social development, which was reflected in patriarchal, tribal, and feudal forms of social organisation.

In these social systems, the relationship between the sexes consisted of absolute unlimited authority for the man and complete subordination for the woman—who was prevented from taking direct part in any form of public work and had therefore no means of achieving economic independence. She was her husband's servant, his personal property, a mute slave shut off from any participation in public life or work and doomed to spend her days in the seclusion of the house in excessively tiring domestic work which completely dulled her sensibilities.

A woman among these backward peoples had no right to work for an independent wage. But this did not in the least prevent her from being employed in various domestic trades without being paid for her work. Whatever she produced was appropriated and sold by her husband.

Women in Central Asia, the Crimea, the Caucasus, Transcaucasus, and in other feudal provinces with a Mohammedan culture, were particularly oppressed. The religious and secular laws of these countries gave man, the head of the family, absolutely unlimited rights over woman and kept her in a position of the most humiliating servility, the most oppressed of all the oppressed.

Custom prohibited a woman from appearing in public places without the escort of her husband or elderly relatives; she was not allowed to talk to other men, nor could she walk in the streets with her face uncovered. As a sign of obedience, girls on reaching the age of nine or ten years put on the *parandja* (in the Caucasus, the *chadra*), a grey covering with a black net over it which enveloped the figure from head to foot. This they were obliged to wear until old age. For his bride, the bridegroom paid a definite sum to her parents, after which she became his personal property.

Soviet power has completely wiped out all limitations in the rights accorded to the national minorities enslaved by Tsarism. The U.S.S.R. is a brotherly union of peoples based on economic, cultural, and political co-operation, and on the principle of planned support and aid for backward peoples, and Soviet policy in the national provinces and republics is directed towards a many-sided economic, industrial, and agrarian development which will transform these recently backward districts into industrial and agrarian provinces with vast possibilities of further development.

This development is accompanied by rapid cultural growth. All the peoples of the Soviet Union, many of whom were completely illiterate under Tsarist rule, are in every possible way encouraged to create their own independent culture.

The Soviet national policy has brought about a complete revolution in the life of the women. By destroying the economic and legal bases of their subjection it has opened for them the doors to public work, to economic independence and cultural development. It has given them the possiblity of complete actual equality with man.

The drawing into production of the women of the national minorities and the complete refashioning of their everyday lives were problems of extraordinary difficulty. To begin with, all innovations met with fierce opposition from feudal and fanatical elements in the population, kulaks and conservatives, who wished to preserve the ancient traditions governing women since all their vital class interests were upheld by them.

Secondly, these traditions had left their mark on the consciousness of the women themselves, and it needed not only new laws but also an enormous amount of mass propaganda and educational work among the women to overcome the age-old customs and ideas, sanctified by religion, which confined a woman to her husband's house.

During the first decade of Soviet power, the organs of government in the national republics (Bashkiria, Azerbaidzhan, Kirghizia, the Central Asiatic republic) passed a series of laws against the traditional customs which had enslaved women. These laws made the struggle for freedom very much easier for the women of these Eastern peoples.

The educational work which accompanied and followed the legislation was organised on a vast scale, and employed methods adapted to conditions of life among Eastern women—methods which took into account their traditional seclusion, complete illiteracy, etc. The chief form taken by this work was the women's clubs, closed to men. These clubs played an enormous part in emancipating the women of the Soviet East. In them the first women's handicraft groups were organised, some of which afterwards developed into large industrial enterprises. Educational courses were opened and advice provided on a

NATIONAL REPUBLICS

variety of topics. In the best women's club in the Union—the Ali Vairamova Club, opened in Baku in 1922—about 10,000 Turkic women were organised.

This club started the first factory in the world entirely run by women, former members of the harem. At the present time there are 1,500 women working in the factory—900 of them Turkic women who have long forgotten their earlier seclusion. The club also organised the first midwifery technical school for Eastern women, as well as courses for typists, for telephone and telegraph operators, for cultural workers, and for collective farm chairmen. There are numerous other clubs doing the same work on a more limited scale. Cultural and educational work is also being organised in even simpler forms—for example, in saklia,[1] reading-huts, and red *jurtas* (in nomad districts).

Large women's conferences and meetings attract many thousands of women who formerly never showed themselves in public. There were 1,600 women's meetings and 20 conferences in Azerbaidzhan in 1923, and 2,000 meetings and 23 conferences in Georgia in 1924.

At the heart of this great educational work was the determined struggle against Mohammedan traditions which prohibited women from

[1] Caucasian hut.

all participation in public life, and thus deprived them of the means of self-development. Notwithstanding the peculiar difficulties of this struggle, decisive victories have been won—particularly during the periods of the First and Second Five-Year Plans. Though certain traditional customs still remain, the great mass of Eastern women have " uncovered " themselves for society, for communal work, and for a cultured life.

The economic development of the national republics and provinces was of enormous importance in speeding up the struggle against the traditional seclusion of women. Soviet policy in these areas during the years of the First and Second Five-Year Plan took the form of a determined struggle against economic and cultural backwardness. This soon made itself felt in an exceptionally rapid rate of industrial and agricultural development and in the permanent settlement of nomad tribes on the land.

Vast numbers of new workers were urgently needed, and an increased number of them had to be recruited from new sources of labour—including women, who had up till then stood outside public work. A wide choice of employment was opened to these secluded women, freed from age-long slavery and social oppression. The very fact that they would now earn an independent wage very much simplified the problem of radically changing their environment, and, indeed, the whole of their lives.

To-day, the part played by women in public work among all the national minorities of the Union is very large. The total number of women workers and employees in national activities (excluding agriculture) in the three republics of Central Asia (Uzbekistan, Turkmenistan, Tadjikistan) was 104,600 in 1932, the last year of the First Five-Year Plan; at the beginning of 1934 it was 115,600; and the proportion of women among the total number of workers increased during this period from 21·6 per cent to 25·8 per cent. In the Transcaucasian Soviet republics (Azerbaidzhan, Armenia, Georgia), the number of women increased from 152,700 on January 1, 1932, to 184,200 on January 1, 1934, with an increase in the proportion of women from 22·9 per cent to 26·7 per cent. In Kazakstan in 1934, 98,600 women were employed in national activities (24·7 per cent of the total number of workers). In the Bashkir republic women constituted 29·2 per cent of the total number of workers in 1935, as compared with 23·9 per cent in 1932; and in the Tartar republic, 35·5 per cent as compared with 30·2 per cent in 1932.

These figures apply to all women working on

the territories of the given republics, and not only native women; but a considerable number of them were native born. In Uzbekistan in 1934, 27·3 per cent of the working women were native born, in Georgia, 45 per cent, in Armenia, 87·7 per cent.

These successes in attracting the women of the national minorities into public work are particularly striking when one compares the proportion of women among all workers with the proportion of women among native-born workers.

Here are the figures for August 1934:

Republic or autonomous province				Percentage of women	
				Among all workers	Among native-born workers
Azerbaidzhan (Soviet Socialist Republic)				25·3	17·8
Georgian	,,	,,	,,	27·6	22·0
Armenian	,,	,,	,,	23·4	23·2
Turkmenistan	,,	,,	,,	24·0	11·7
Uzbekistan	,,	,,	,,	26·2	18·4
Bashkiria (autonomous)	,,		,,	26·5	22·0
Kirghizian	,,	,,	,,	21·1	18·1
Daghestan	,,	,,	,,	27·0	15·4
Chuvash A.R.	,,	,,	,,	25·5	23·0
Crimean	,,	,,	,,	30·6	32·2
Mordovian	,,	,,	,,	24·0	25·8

This table clearly shows that in some of the national republics (Azerbaidzhan, Georgia, Turkmenistan, Uzbekistan) native-born women who

NATIONAL REPUBLICS

formerly had taken no part in public work had, by 1934, been drawn into production to a somewhat lesser degree than women of other nationalities living in the same republics (chiefly Russian women). However, in other republics (Armenia, Chuvash A.R.) this inequality has been almost overcome; and in the Crimean and Mordovian autonomous republics, native-born women are in a majority among women workers.

In order fully to appreciate these remarkable successes we must remember that they have been achieved in an extremely short time. As late as 1926, according to data of the all-Union census, there were 112 Uzbek women engaged in productive work, 1 Turkic woman, and 4 Tadjik.

In industry, the women of the national minorities are chiefly employed in textile and sewing factories. But an increasing number of women are entering other branches of industry also. There were only five women in the metal-working industries of the Tartar republic in 1926; in 1935, women already constituted 28·4 per cent of the total number of workers. In the chemical industry, the proportion of women among workers increased during this period from 10·3 per cent to 38·5 per cent. We have also been greatly successful in drawing masses of women into agriculture. In 1935, 23 per cent of all the work done on collective farms in Uzbekistan was performed by women; in Turkmenistan, 27 per cent.

The introduction into industry of women of the national minorities was accompanied by an advance in their cultural level, and by a much higher standard of technical training for skilled work.

We have already noted that the Soviet Government inherited a population that was 70 per cent illiterate. Among the oppressed nationalities this percentage was even higher. Among Tartars it was 81·9 per cent; among White Russians, 88·7 per cent; among the Chuvash people, 94·4 per cent; among the Circassians, 91·2 per cent; among the inhabitants of Kabardino, 96·6 per cent. There were even fewer literate women than men, and in a number of districts there were no literate women at all. Among the Turkic women in 1926, 0·2 per cent were literate; among Kirghiz women, 0·3 per cent.

As a result of the colossal work that has been carried out and is still in progress, the number of illiterates in these backward republics declined rapidly. To-day, a number of national republics which were completely illiterate under Tsarist rule are almost completely literate (Ingushetia, Chuvash, Adigea, etc.); and liquidation of illiteracy among women is being achieved at an increasingly rapid rate in the national republics.

NATIONAL REPUBLICS

In Azerbaidzhan in 1920 there were 3,016 literate Turkic people, including 374 women; in 1932 there were already 396,689 literates, including 150,000 women. The immediate task is complete literacy for the population in the near future.

In Turkmenistan there were in all 24 literate women in 1926; in 1932 the percentage of literate women had risen to 18 in rural districts (in the mountain villages) and 72 in the towns. In the Tartar republic, only 5 per cent of the women were literate under Tsarist rule; to-day about 70 per cent of them can read and write.

The urge of the workers of the East towards knowledge—their desire for literacy—is eloquently shown by the fact that the annual plan for liquidating illiteracy in the national republics is systematically over-fulfilled.

No less significant are statistics showing the growth of club work in the national republics. Clubs in the Soviet Union (reading-huts in the villages, factory clubs, people's houses of culture, palaces of culture) are centres of extra-school cultural and educational work among the adult population. They are also the chief centres for fostering creative initiative among the masses in all branches of culture. The growth of club work is thus a particularly reliable indication of the growth of culture among the population.

The following table shows the development of clubs and similar institutions in the chief national republics of the Union.

	Reading-huts	
	1928–29	1933–34
Transcaucasus	801	1,407
Uzbekistan	554	3,471
Turkmenistan	77	248
Tadjikistan	21	317

	Clubs, people's houses and palaces of culture	
	1928–29	1933–34
Transcaucasus	1,071	2,093
Uzbekistan	802	3,852
Turkmenistan	128	353
Tadjikistan	32	379

These figures need no comment. They speak of the rapid growth of cultural institutions in all the republics of the Soviet East. And not so very long ago the inhabitants of these provinces had not the remotest idea of what a club was. They had neither access to knowledge nor the opportunity for leisure. Even the alphabet was denied to them.

Remarkable successes, too, have been achieved in drawing girls into the general schools. In 1927, girls constituted 24·4 per cent of the total number of pupils in the general schools of Uzbekistan; in 1935–36 they constituted 40·2 per cent. In Turkmenistan, the percentage of girls among the pupils increased during this period from

29 per cent to 42·5 per cent. We find similar achievements in other national republics. In some of them (Crimea, Buriat-Mongolia) girls form half the total number of pupils in the general schools—a larger proportion than in the Union as a whole.

It is particularly noteworthy that in the rural districts of these republics, where in the recent past women knew nothing of either letters or schools, the number of girls in the schools has grown with exceptional rapidity. In the village schools of Turkmenistan and Uzbekistan, for example, girls constituted 10 per cent of the total number of pupils in 1927–31; in 1935–36 the proportion was about 40 per cent.

The widespread attraction of women of the national minorities into special schools for training skilled workers is a magnificent result of Soviet governmental policy. In 1933, in many of the national republics, girls constituted almost the same proportion of the pupils in the factory schools for training skilled workers as they did in similar schools in Russia proper or the Ukraine. Women, for example, constituted 27·1 per cent of the Chuvash pupils in factory schools; in the Bashkirian schools the proportion was 24·8 per cent. The percentage of girls among pupils of all nationalities was 27·7; among Russians, 29·1; among Ukrainians, 24·9. The lower percentage of girls in Ukrainian factory schools may be explained by the industrial character of these schools. Most of them are schools for heavy industry, in which women are employed to a lesser degree than in light industry. In a number of national republics the proportion of girls to the total number of pupils was in 1933 still considerably less than the average number of women in schools throughout the whole of the Union, but the figure was none the less quite high.

The number of preparatory courses for training women of the national minorities for skilled work is also increasing. Thus, for example, women constituted 39·5 per cent of the pupils at the Central Institute of Labour in Uzbekistan in 1933; and more than 25 per cent in the shortened courses. In the courses connected with the People's Commissariat for Agriculture in Kazakstan, more than 33 per cent of the pupils were women.

Women of the national minorities have everywhere been encouraged to take the State technical examination. But what is particularly creditable is that the woman of the East, only yesterday a prisoner in her husband's house, where no spark of knowledge ever reached her, has in a short time won a firm place for herself in the middle and higher professional and technical schools which prepare highly qualified specialists, technicians, engineers, agronomists, etc. In 1933–34 women constituted 40 per cent of the Tartar pupils in technical schools (as compared with 44 per cent among Russians) and 36·1 per cent in the universities (as compared with 35·6 per cent among Russians). Of Bashkirian pupils women supplied 36 per cent in the technical schools and 22·7 per cent in the universities. Corresponding figures for the women of Buriat-Mongolia are 39·8 per cent in the technical schools and 24 per cent in the universities; for women of the mountainous nationalities, 18 per cent and 20·4 per cent; for Turkoman women, 16·6 per cent and 14·3 per cent; for Tadjik women, 18·8 per cent and 14·1 per cent, and so on.

Increased culture and technical knowledge have meant that women of the national minorities have won speedy promotion to various kinds of qualified work. Many skilled workers from the ranks of Turkoman, Georgian, and Tartar women have distinguished themselves as the best shock-workers in the industry.

The oil-worker Milonova, in the tenth compressor group at the Ileych Bay in Baku, is considered to be the best industrial worker in Azerbaidzhan, and has received special bonuses on seven occasions. The Trade Union of Oil Workers has awarded her the Certificate of

Merit for outstanding work in fulfilling the oil plan.

For months, Fatima Babaeva, a Turkic oil-worker in the third group of Baku enterprises, regularly over-fulfilled the production plan. She has received many prizes, and has been proposed by the Trade Union of Oil Workers for a Certificate of Merit.

The Georgian woman Tugulia Egorovna Shengelia, who rose from an ordinary unskilled worker to the position of instructor in the Tiflis silk factory, has several inventions to her credit, and the Soviet Government has awarded her the Order of the Red Banner of Labour for outstanding work.

Mastery of the technique of production has enabled women of the national minorities to participate in the Stakhanov movement which has spread throughout the Union. In the Tartar republic, for example, Salakhutdinova, a weaver in the Kazan Flax Combinat, works on four looms and has almost doubled both her output and her earnings. Romanova, a dresser in the Kazan fur factory, has achieved a record in her work by systematically over-fulfilling her plan by more than 300 per cent.

The work of the women of the national minorities in agriculture has produced even more striking results. In the Tartar republic many groups of qualified women agricultural workers have been trained, and during the last two years 938 of them have qualified as tractor drivers, 56 as combine drivers, 1,448 as brigadiers of field-brigades, and 854 as managers of live-stock farms.

In the agricultural campaign of 1935, women of the national minorities produced brilliant examples of outstanding work in all branches of agriculture. In the Tartar republic, many hundreds of collective farmers mastered Stakhanovite methods of work in grain-farming. Many Tartar tractor-drivers ploughed more than 1,000 hectares during the season, the average norm for the Union being 400 hectares. Excellent results were obtained by Tartar, Buriat, and Kazak women in live-stock farming. For example, the Buriat woman Endineeva, a milkmaid, has not lost a single calf through sickness in six years, and has received fourteen prizes for work on a collective farm. The Kazak milkmaids Utabaeva and Tarmantan and many others have achieved similar successes.

One may say that in the national republics the raising of live-stock is passing chiefly into the hands of women. They have learnt how to manage the farms well, how to look after young animals, and how to raise them properly.

Particularly striking are the achievements

of the women of the Soviet Eastern nationalities in cotton-growing. In 1935 the Soviet Union gathered a record harvest of cotton. The collective farm cotton-growers of Uzbekistan, Kazakstan, Karakalpakia, Tadjikistan, Turkmenistan and Azerbaidzhan produced hitherto unknown harvests of cotton—harvests " entirely unknown in capitalist countries, and of which no one had ever heard before Soviet collectivisation." Formerly people thought that 10–15 centners per acre was a good yield for the American varieties of cotton. In 1935, many of the collective farmers gathered harvests of 25, 30, 40, and even more centners per hectare. For the best quality of Egyptian cotton, 8 – 10 centners per hectare was considered a record harvest; in 1935 many Soviet cotton-fields produced a harvest of 15 – 20 centners per hectare.

The women shock-workers of the cotton industry—Uzbeks, Turkomans, Tadjiks, and Turkic women—did much to make these successes possible. In 1935 many of them came to the fore in the ranks of the Union's most distinguished workers and were decorated by the Government. Twenty Eastern women were awarded the Order of Lenin for achieving a harvest of not less than 15 centners of Egyptian cotton per hectare and 30 and more centners of American cotton. Six women were awarded the Order of the Red

Banner of Labour, and seven the Order of the Sign of Honour for far exceeding the average yield for a cotton harvest. Among these women we must single out the Turkoman women, Ogul Guzel Bakhbid, detachment leader on the Bolshevik collective farm in the Bairam-Ali district, who achieved a harvest of 50 centners of American cotton per hectare; and Gul Nabat, detachment leader of the Volunteer collective farm in the Stalin district, who achieved a harvest of 25 centners of Egyptian cotton per hectare.

Not a few of these Eastern women are working as specialists, engineers, and technicians. There are 132 Tartar women engineers working in industrial concerns in the Tartar republic. Many women work as engineers in the Transcaucasian republics and some of them have become famous throughout the Union.

Kemar Ragimova works in the seventh group of the Ordjonikidze Oil Works in Baku. She has shown herself to be an extremely energetic engineer who systematically over-fulfils the plan for oil. In the past she endured all the humiliations common to Eastern women. When she was thirteen the *chadra* was put on her head, and a few months later she was given in marriage. Her first child was born when she was fifteen. Before the Revolution, Kemar led the ordinary life of the Eastern woman, but with the establishment of Soviet power she broke away from ancient traditions. She began to show herself on the street, joined a club, and, in 1926, discarded the *chadra* and began to study, first at a general educational course, then in a Rabfak, then at the Industrial Academy, from which she graduated as an engineer at the age of thirty-six.

In 1934, Kemar was elected to the Baku Soviet. In a speech at the election meeting she said: " There was a time when people believed in miracles. But real miracles are being performed by the Soviet Government. If I had said to anybody before that I was going to be an engineer they would have put me in a madhouse. And now I am an engineer ! "

Another outstanding engineer is the Georgian woman Arusya Aretunova. After finishing the preparatory training course with great difficulty, she took the engineer's course at the Mining Academy in Moscow, mastering fully at the same time the Russian tongue. In 1929, as one of the most diligent students, she was sent to America to study the incandescent-thermic working of metals at the Ford factory.

As the first Soviet woman engineer in America she aroused no little interest: people came to look at her and found it hard to believe that she was an engineer. But in America, too, she showed outstanding gifts, and Ford expressed high opinion about her as a talented engineer with a promising future.

In 1933, Aretunova entered the thermic department of the Calibre factory—a department which played a decisive part in the production of the factory as a whole. Here she organised the work in an exemplary manner. The section, which had fallen behind in the fulfilment of its plan, began systematically to over-fulfil it. For 1934, it fulfilled the production plan to the extent of 120 per cent. The productivity of labour reached 170 per cent as compared with the standard for 1933. It continued to work at this level in 1935.

Not a few Eastern women are now at the head of industrial enterprises. The Turkic woman Vegil Radjalova, organised, in 1920, the first women's sewing artel, which in 1929 was extended into a large sewing factory with more than 2,000 workers. Radjalova is now director of this factory. Gasiza Sagandinova, director of the No. 3 Kazan sewing factory, was awarded the Red Banner of Labour by the Government for her good work.

In the collective farms many women have been promoted to leading posts. Here they work as chairmen, members of managing bodies, and heads of farming brigades. The majority of dairy-farm managers are women.

Women of the national minorities are also winning places for themselves as teachers and doctors. The majority of primary school teachers in the Transcaucasus in 1935 were women—in the towns 83 per cent, in the villages 45 per cent. A large part of the teaching staff in the secondary schools were also women (46 per cent in the towns, 19 per cent in the villages). In Uzbekistan the corresponding percentages are equally high. Half of all the teachers in secondary schools in the towns are women.

In the Tartar republic before the Revolution there were in all 8 women doctors, not one of whom was native born. Now there are 743, of whom 30 per cent are native born. About the same proportion of Tartar women is to be found among the assistant medical personnel. We also find women of the national minorities engaged in academic work as professors, assistant professors, and scientific workers. Young women study in the institutes of Red professors and do post-graduate work in the universities and research institutes.

An enormous amount of work has been done in the national republics in freeing women from domestic cares. Communal services for the care and education of children, crèches and kindergartens—entirely unknown before the Revolution and incompatible with the former mode

NATIONAL REPUBLICS

of life of the Eastern peoples—have been rapidly developed in the Soviet Eastern republics. Here their rate of development exceeds that of crèches and kindergartens in the Soviet Union as a whole, as is shown by the following figures:

	Number of places in thousands In crèches	
	1928	1934
Transcaucasus	1·2	65·6
Uzbekistan	0·9	121·6
Turkmenistan	0·4	39·9
Tadjikistan	0·0	27·6

	Number of places in thousands In kindergartens	
	1927–28	1934–35
Transcaucasus	11·2	240·7
Uzbekistan	3·9	163·4
Turkmenistan	2·7	42·0
Tadjikistan	0·0	5·9

We see that the number of children served by crèches during the period 1928–34 in the Transcaucasian republics increased almost 55 times; in the republics of Central Asia by 145 times. The rate of growth of the kindergarten system is no less striking. This rapid development of communal forms of child education was the decisive factor in attracting Eastern women into public work and consolidating their position in industry. It also gave them time for study and other cultural pursuits.

The exceptional care given to mother and

child by the Soviet State is evident in the widespread development of lying-in service in the national republics. If in the whole of the Union the number of beds in the medically equipped lying-in homes has increased by six times as compared with 1913, it has grown even more rapidly in the national republics. The number of beds in lying-in homes in Turkmenistan has increased fifteen times; in Uzbekistan sixteen times. A great number of institutions for the care of mother and child have been organised in the national republics during the years of the Soviet régime. Formerly no such institutions existed. All these services provide women of the national minorities with civilised hygienic conditions for child-bearing and the feeding and rearing of children.

The raising of the marriage age for women did much to destroy the old mode of life in the national republics. In former times, women in Central Asia, in the Caucasus and the Crimea, were often given in marriage when they were twelve to fifteen years old. According to the law of the R.S.F.S.R., eighteen years is the minimum age for marriage. In the Ukrainian Socialist Soviet Republic the legal marriage age for women is somewhat lower—sixteen years. In actual fact, a noticeable advance in the marriage age for women is one of the phenomena common to all the national republics and to the Union as a whole. The horrible custom of parents giving in marriage (in fact, actually selling) young girls, often physically immature, who were obliged to submit patiently to their parents' will, is passing into the sphere of legend in the Soviet Union.

But it would be incorrect to pretend that these ancient traditions in the life of Eastern women have been completely stamped out, or that they have disappeared without leaving any trace. There are still cases of girls being kidnapped in Central Asia and the Caucasus; still despotic husbands and marriage to minors. One may still frequently see in the towns and villages of these national districts women in *parandjas*, which symbolise their seclusion from society and public life. Not a few girls still have to fight bravely for a free independent life; for the right to marry whom they please; for the right to study and to work.

The Communist Party, the Komsomol, the organs of the Soviet State, and the trade unions, wage active war against ancient traditions which survive in the consciousness of women and in the customs of the people and hamper the growth of a new life. At the end of 1935 fifteen conferences of young women were organised by the Komsomol in all the most important national republics. These conferences played an enormous part in the fight for freedom. Uzbek, Chechen, and Tadjik girls who attended them described the magnificent achievements of the women of the national minorities in the struggle for a free cultured life, and told of the difficulties with which they had to contend. As an outcome of these conferences, increased educational work is being conducted at the present time among girls in the national republics, and legal penalties are exacted on all who infringe upon their legal rights.

In conclusion, let us point to the exceptional growth of social and political activity among women of the national minorities.

In Uzbekistan, the percentage of women who recorded votes at the election of deputies to the soviets rose from 7·8 per cent in 1926 to 69·4 in 1934; in Turkmenistan, from 2·5 in 1927 to 73·5 in 1934; in Tadjikistan, from 22 in 1929 to 72·5 in 1934.

There are women members and women chairmen of soviets, in the administrative organs of the trade union movement, and in other social organisations. Women also occupy a number of responsible posts in Government State administration. The vice-chairmen of the Central Executive Committees of Turkmenistan and Uzbekistan are women.

The profound effect of the upheaval in the

NATIONAL REPUBLICS

mode of life and consciousness of these women of the national minorities is vividly reflected in the development of social and political activity among them. Vast numbers of women who formerly lived weighed down by oppression, in a sad, hopeless condition amounting to slavery, are developing into conscious builders of a new society, of a new culture, national in form, socialist in content. This is the chief outcome of the magnificent achievements of the Soviet Union in the sphere of women's work and life in the national republics.

CONCLUSION

WE HAVE FOLLOWED point by point the measures carried out by the Soviet Government towards securing the real equality of women with men in society, in cultural life, and in production.

The present stage of social development in the Soviet Union—the stage of building a classless society—is characterised by an increased interest in the needs and demands of every human being, in problems connected with his personal well-being and cultural development.

Special attention and special respect are paid to the woman as worker and the woman as mother. In the Soviet Union there is no contradiction between motherhood and participation in industrial work and social activity. On the contrary, they exist in harmonious conjunction and mutually complement each other. At the present time, as a result of magnificent achievements in the assimilation of women into public work and social life, and of increasing material prosperity, the task of ensuring happy motherhood for every woman is one of the most

CONCLUSION

important social problems in the Soviet Union.

We are already acquainted with details of the vast net of institutions that exists for the care of mother and child. Every year the number of these institutions has increased; and during the next few years they are to be developed at a particularly rapid rate. The number of crèches, both in town and country, is to be doubled during the period 1936–38; and in the course of these three years about 5,000,000 new places will be made available in them. Kindergartens in town and country during this period will grow by 2,270,000 places—that is, almost threefold. In the collective farms a vast new system of seasonal kindergartens is to be developed which will serve 23,000,000 children. In 1938, in the busy agricultural months, these seasonal services will look after all the children on the collective farms.

In the first chapter we quoted the substance of the new law for the care of mothers, which considerably increases State aid, extends lying-in services, and makes provision for a series of other measures no less important in protecting the mother's rights and interests. The Soviet mother need not worry about her children, the ones she has and the ones she will bring into the world. She knows that the State will give her every aid in their upbringing and education. The growth

CONCLUSION

of well-being among the population and the vast development of all forms of State aid for mothers have made the legal prohibition of abortion very opportune.

Abortions were temporarily allowed because women were living under difficult material conditions. To-day, these difficulties have been overcome, and there is no longer any reason for permitting abortions, which are harmful to women and often hinder the creation of a strong, healthy family.

It would be incorrect to think that the chief aim of this prohibition is to increase the birthrate and the annual growth of the population. In this respect the Soviet Union has nothing to fear. At the present time the population of the Soviet Union increases by 3,000,000 yearly. The birth-rate is growing steadily, the death-rate declining, which makes for a further increase in the annual growth of the population.

Nobody in the Soviet Union can doubt that the State is capable of feeding this growing army of workers and providing them with regular employment. The rapid planned development of all branches of national economy ensures the further growth of national well-being, and excludes the possibility of a recrudescence of unemployment in the U.S.S.R., however large the annual increase in the number of workers

CONCLUSION

may be. The firm conviction among Soviet workers that their children will be given a happy childhood and a happy life is a powerful stimulus to a high birth-rate. The prohibition of abortion is above all an effort to safeguard women's health and to protect them from the painful and frequently incurable consequences of this operation. But there is another side to this problem. One of the reasons for the widespread practice of abortion was that frivolous attitude towards marriage and parental responsibilities which naturally accompanies a disorderly sex life. But this attitude has nothing in common with the ethics and standards of behaviour of a Soviet citizen. Fatherhood and motherhood are respected in the Soviet Union as personal and civic virtues; and men and women with a frivolous attitude towards married life, who will not accept the responsibility of bearing and educating children, are unanimously condemned by public opinion. The prohibition of abortion in the Soviet Union is the legal means of fighting this criminal attitude towards marriage and married life.

The struggle against abortions and the general Soviet policy regarding the protection of motherhood and easing the burden of maternal responsibilities show what enormous significance is attached to the creation of strong, healthy

CONCLUSION

families which will educate new generations of Soviet citizens.

Before the Soviet woman stretches the boundless horizon of a happy, healthy life. Motherhood is essential for the complete fulfilment of woman. It is for this reason that the care of women occupies such an exceptionally prominent place in the general social policy of the Soviet State, which is designed to harmonise with the widest possible assimilation of women into socialist construction and their fullest cultural and social development.

APPENDIX

APPENDIX I

EXTRACT FROM CODE OF LABOUR LAWS OF THE U.S.S.R.

(Chapter xiii)

WORK FOR WOMEN AND MINORS

129. It is forbidden to employ women and minors, under eighteen, in especially strenuous and harmful—for the health—industries and underground work.

A list of especially strenuous and harmful work as well as record norms for carrying heavy loads for women and for minors is determined by the Commissariat of Heavy Industry with the consent of the All-Russian Central Council of Trade Unions.

130. Women and those under eighteen are not permitted to do night-work.

Note. The Commissariat of Heavy Industry, with agreement of the All-Russian Central Council of Trade Unions, retains the right to permit grown-up women to do night-work in those branches of industry where it is deemed absolutely necessary.

131. Pregnant and nursing mothers are not permitted to work overtime or at night.

In those enterprises where there is the seven-hour-day work, pregnant women, beginning with the sixth

APPENDIX

month, and nursing women during the first six months of nursing are not permitted to do night-work (May 27, 1929; Code No. 40, article 414).

133. Beginning with the fifth month of pregnancy, it is not permitted to send women on business trips outside of their permanent place of work without their consent thereto.

134. Besides the general existing recess periods (article 100) there must be established additional recess periods for nursing women to nurse their babies. The exact times of such recess periods are established by the place of work itself; such nursing periods must be permitted not less than within an interval of $3\frac{1}{2}$ hours and must last not less than a half-hour.

The time of such nursing periods are not deducted from the working time.

APPENDIX II

DECREE ON THE PROHIBITION OF ABORTIONS, Etc.

(Decision of the C.E.C. and the Council of People's Commissars of the U.S.S.R.)

On the Prohibition of Abortions.
Increase of Material Aid to Women Giving Birth.
Establishment of State Aid to Large Families.
Broadening of the Network of Maternity Homes, Nurseries and Kindergartens.
Strengthening of the Criminal Penalty for Non-Payment of Alimony.
And on Certain Changes in the Legislation on Divorces.

The October Socialist Revolution which laid the foundation for the abolition of all class exploitation, for the abolition of the classes themselves, at the same time laid the foundation for the complete and final emancipation of women.

In no country in the world does woman enjoy as complete equality in all branches of political, social, and family life as in the U.S.S.R.

In no country in the world does woman, as a mother and a citizen who bears the great and responsible duty of giving birth to and bringing up citizens, enjoy the

APPENDIX

same respect and protection of the law as in the U.S.S.R.

However, the economic breakdown of the country which took place during the first years after the civil war and the armed intervention, and the inadequate cultural level of the women inherited from the pre-revolutionary epoch did not enable them at once to make full use of the rights accorded to them by the law and to perform, without fear of the future, their duties as citizens and mothers responsible for the birth and early education of their children. In this connection the Soviet power permitted on November 18, 1920, the practice of abortions (artificial interruption of pregnancy) for women so long as, as the People's Commissariat of Health and the People's Commissariat of Justice wrote, " the moral heritages of the past and the difficult economic conditions of the present still force a section of the women to submit to this operation " (Code of Laws, No. 90, p. 471).

Back in 1913 Lenin wrote that class-conscious workers are " unquestionable enemies of neo-Malthusianism, this tendency for the philistine couple, pigeon-brained and selfish, who murmur fearfully: May God help us to keep our own bodies and souls together: s for children, it is best to be without them."

But, while rebelling against abortions as a social evil, Lenin considered the mere legislative banning of abortions clearly inadequate to combat them. Moreover, he pointed out that under conditions of capitalism these laws only reflect the " hypocrisy of the ruling classes " as they " do not heal the sores of capitalism but make them particularly malignant, particularly

APPENDIX

painful to the oppressed masses" (Volume 16, pp. 498–99).

Only under conditions of socialism, where exploitation of man by man does not exist and where woman is an equal member of society while the progressing improvement of the material well-being of the toilers constitutes a law of social development, is it possible seriously to organise the struggle against abortions by prohibitive laws as well as by other means.

The abolition of capitalist exploitation in the U.S.S.R., the growth of the material well-being and the gigantic growth of the political and cultural level of the toilers make it possible to raise the question of a revision of the decision of the People's Commissariats of Health and Justice of November 18, 1920.

Necessary material provision for women and their children, State aid to large families, the utmost development of the network of maternity homes, nurseries, kindergartens, legislative establishment of a minimum of sums which the father of a child must pay for its upkeep when husband and wife live apart, on the one hand, and prohibition of abortions on the other, coupled with an increase in the penalty for wilful non-payment of the means for the maintenance of the children, awarded by a court, and the introduction of certain changes in the legislation on divorces for the purpose of combating a light-minded attitude towards the family and family obligations—such are the roads which must be followed in order to solve this important problem affecting the entire population. In this respect, the Soviet Government responds to numerous statements made by toiling women.

APPENDIX

In connection with the above, and taking into consideration certain remarks made by citizens during the discussion of the draft, the C.E.C. and the Council of People's Commissars of the U.S.S.R. DECIDE:

I

ON PROHIBITION OF ABORTIONS

1. In view of the proven harm of abortions, to forbid the performance of abortions both in hospitals and special health institutions, and in the homes of doctors and private homes of pregnant women. The performance of abortions shall be allowed exclusively in those cases when the continuation of pregnancy endangers the life or threatens serious injury to the health of the pregnant woman and equally when a serious disease of the parents can be inherited, and only under hospital or maternity home conditions.

2. For the performance of abortions outside a hospital or in a hospital under conditions violating the above provisions, the doctor performing the abortion shall be criminally punishable to the extent of one to two years of imprisonment, while for the performance of abortions under insanitary conditions or by persons who have no special medical education a criminal penalty of no less than three years' imprisonment shall be fixed.

3. For compelling a woman to undergo an abortion, a criminal penalty of two years' imprisonment shall be fixed.

APPENDIX

4. In relation to pregnant women undergoing an abortion in violation of the said prohibition, to establish as a criminal penalty a social reprimand, and in the event of a repetition of the violation of the law on the prohibition of abortions, a fine up to 300 roubles.

II

ON INCREASING MATERIAL AID BY THE STATE TO WOMEN GIVING BIRTH AND ON ESTABLISHING STATE AID TO LARGE FAMILIES

5. In order to improve the material position of mothers, both working women and employees insured in the organs of social insurance, to increase the allowance issued from the State social insurance funds for the purpose of procuring the necessary articles of infant care, from 32 roubles to 45 roubles.

6. To increase the allowance issued to the mother for nursing the infant, from 5 roubles to 10 roubles a month.

7. In relation to uninsured toiling women—members of co-operative artels and enterprises—to establish that the said allowances be issued by the co-operative mutual aid funds on the same basis.

8. To abolish the limitation fixed by the code of labour laws for women employees (article 132), making them equal to working women in regard to the length of the leave accorded prior to and after childbirth (56 days prior to and 56 days after childbirth).

APPENDIX

9. To establish a criminal penalty for refusal to employ women for reasons of pregnancy, for reducing their wages on the same grounds, providing in the law the obligation of preserving for the pregnant woman, while transferring her to lighter work, her former wages based on earnings for the last six months' work.

10. To establish a State allowance for mothers of large families—for those having six children, an annual allowance of 2,000 roubles for five years for each subsequent child from the day of its birth, while for mothers having ten children one State allowance of 5,000 roubles on the birth of each subsequent child and an annual allowance of 3,000 roubles for a period of four years following the child's first birthday. To extend this article of the law also to those families who at the moment of the publication of the law have the required number of children.

III

ON EXTENSION OF THE NETWORK OF MATERNITY HOMES

To instruct the People's Commissariats of Health of the constituent republics:

11. In order to provide medical assistance in special maternity homes for all women giving birth in cities, industrial and district centres, to establish and open by January 1, 1939, 11,000 new maternity beds, of which, in addition to the 4,200 beds provided by the 1936 plan, there are to be established:

APPENDIX

In 1936	2,000 beds
In 1937	4,000 ,,
In 1938	5,000 ,,

12. In order to extend medical service to women giving birth in rural localities, to provide and put into use 32,000 maternity beds, of which 16,000 beds in the maternity wards of village hospitals shall be at the expense of the State budget and 16,000 beds by organising collective farm maternity homes, 75 per cent of the cost of their organisation to be put at the expense of collective farms and 25 per cent at the expense of the State budget.

These are to include:

In 1936—in addition to the 4,300 maternity beds in village hospitals and the 5,000 beds in collective farm maternity homes scheduled by the 1936 plan—4,000 beds in hospitals, and 4,000 beds in collective farm maternity homes.

In 1937—6,000 beds in hospitals and 6,000 beds in collective farm maternity homes.

1938—6,000 beds in hospitals and 6,000 beds in collective farm maternity homes.

13. In order to provide women giving birth who are not served by lying-in hospitals with obstetrical assistance in their homes, to open by January 1, 1939, 14,400 new obstetrical stations of which 2,700 obstetrical stations are to be opened in the villages and 1,370 obstetricians appointed to the new collective farm maternity homes in 1936, 5,000 obstetrical stations in the villages and 2,000 obstetricians at the new collective

APPENDIX

farm maternity homes in 1937, 6,700 obstetrical stations in the villages and 2,000 obstetricians at the new collective farm maternity homes in 1938.

IV

ON THE EXTENSION OF THE NETWORK OF NURSERIES

14. To double by January 1, 1939, the existing network of nursery beds for children in the cities, state farms, workers' settlements and on the railways, increasing their total number to 800,000 beds by putting into service:

In 1936, in addition to the 34,000 beds provided by the 1936 plan .. .. 100,000 new beds
In 1937 .. .. .. 150,000 ,, ,,
In 1938 .. .. .. 150,000 ,, ,,

Total .. 400,000 ,, ,,

15. To double by January 1, 1939, the existing network of nursery beds both in permanent and seasonal collective farm nurseries in rural localities, increasing the number of beds in permanent nurseries by 500,000 and in seasonal nurseries by 4,000,000 beds, including:

In 1936, in addition to the 70,000 beds in permanent collective farm nurseries scheduled by the 1936 plan .. .. 100,000 beds

APPENDIX

in seasonal nurseries in addition to the one million beds, according to the 1936 plan	500,000 beds
In 1937 in permanent collective farm nurseries	200,000 ,,
in seasonal nurseries	1,500,000 ,,
In 1938 in permanent collective farm nurseries	200,000 ,,
in seasonal nurseries	2,000,000 ,,

The People's Commissariats of Health of the Union republics and the territory, province and district executive committees are to supervise the development of the above network of nurseries.

16. In cities and in industrial centres, beginning January 1, 1937, work in nursery schools is to be in two shifts, to last 16 hours a day, including the rest days.

17. To instruct the People's Commissariats of Health of the Union republics to secure the appropriate personnel for the newly opened institutions by allotting 15,000,000 roubles in addition to the appropriations made for the training of the intermediate medical personnel.

18. To instruct the People's Commissariats of Health of the Union republics to build during three years so as to complete by January 1, 1939, an additional 800 new dairy kitchens in the cities, industrial and district centres for the feeding of 1,500,000 children under three years of age and to open:

In 1936—30 kitchens of the first category (at an estimated cost of 83,000 roubles each).

APPENDIX

    100 kitchens of the second category (at an estimated cost of 65,000 roubles each).

In 1937—70 kitchens of the first category.

    200 kitchens of the second category.

In 1938—100 kitchens of the first category.

    300 kitchens of the second category.

V

ON ENLARGING NETWORK OF KINDERGARTENS

    19. To triple the functioning network of permanent kindergartens in cities, factory settlements, and on railways within three years, bringing it up to 2,100,000 places by January 1, 1939 (as against 700,000 places in the present network of kindergartens); and at state farms, plants and institutions in village localities, up to 300,000 places, as against 130,000 places of the present network, for which purpose the following must be built and put into operation:

In 1936: In cities, factory settlements, and on railways, in addition to 250,000 places planned according to the 1936 programme	150,000 places
At state farms and at enterprises and institutions in village localities, the plan for the increase of kindergartens in 1936 is to be left at the former	60,000 ,,

APPENDIX

In 1937: In cities, factory settlements, and on railways .. ..   300,000 places
at state farms and at enterprises and institutions in village localities   60,000 „
In 1938: In cities, factory settlements, and on railways .. ..   700,000 „
at state farms and at enterprises and institutions in village localities   50,000 „

20. To open permanent kindergartens, with 700,000 places, at collective farms, in addition to the existing network of 400,000 places, by January 1, 1939, as follows:

In 1936, supplementary to the planned 150,000 for 1936, 50,000 places (total—200,000 places)
In 1937 .. ..   240,000 places
In 1938 .. ..   260,000 „

By the same date to provide all children on collective farms with seasonal playgrounds for children of pre-school age, for which purpose the following must be built:

In 1936 (according to the 1936 plan) .. ..   4,500,000 places
In 1937 .. ..   7,800,000 „
In 1938 .. ..   10,700,000 „

Supervision of the development of the network of kindergartens and seasonal playgrounds for children of pre-school age in village localities is to be turned over

APPENDIX

to the People's Commissariats of Education of the Union republics and to the territorial, province and district executive committees.

21. To obligate the People's Commissariats of Education of the Union republics to train, as early as in the second half of 1936, 50,000 teachers for the kindergartens which are to be opened, releasing 35,000,000 roubles for this purpose in addition to the 1936 grants for the training of cadres for new kindergartens, according to the budgets of the People's Commissariats of Education of the Union republics.

VI

ON CHANGING THE SYSTEM OF SUPERVISION OF KINDERGARTENS

22. To amend the decision of the Council of People's Commissars of the U.S.S.R. of July 6, 1935 (Code of Laws, No. 35, Statute 309), on concentrating the leadership and management of all kindergartens under the systems of the People's Commissariats of Education of the Union republics, turning over to the jurisdiction of the economic People's Commissariats, institutions, and enterprises those kindergartens which have children of workers and employees of these institutions and enterprises, and leaving under the jurisdiction of the People's Commissariats of Education only those kindergartens which serve small institutions and enterprises that do not have their own kindergartens. To place direct leadership of the kindergartens under the administration of the enterprise or institution where the

APPENDIX

kindergarten is organised, with the participation of the factory and plant trade union committees and Young Communist League organisations of these plants and institutions. To reserve for the People's Commissariats of Education of the Union republics general pedagogical leadership, control of the correct structure of the network of the kindergartens and the training of pedagogical cadres.

The Council of People's Commissars of the U.S.S.R. is to determine the method of transferring and financing the kindergartens, and also the method of construction and financing new kindergartens in connection with the newly established system of supervision and management of kindergartens.

VII

ON FINANCING THE ABOVE MEASURES

23. In accordance with this decision, to assign, over and above the sum allocated for 1936 in the State and local budgets and the social insurance budget, 1,481,300,000 roubles for maternity homes, midwife stations, nurseries, dairies and kindergartens, additional for 1936, 692,800,000 roubles for the construction and development of the network of these institutions, increasing the general amount assigned in 1936 to 2,174,100,000 roubles as against 875,000,000 roubles in 1935.

From the above-mentioned 692,800,000 roubles to use on the construction of:

APPENDIX

		Roubles
(a)	Maternity beds in cities	22,200,000
(b)	Maternity beds in villages	23,800,000
(c)	Children's nurseries in cities	*320,000,000
(d)	Kindergartens in cities	*221,000,000
(e)	Dairy kitchens	9,000,000
	Total for construction	596,000,000

On operating expenses:

(a)	For maintenance of the newly opened maternity beds and midwife stations	5,000,000
(b)	For maintenance until the end of 1936 of newly built children's nurseries	11,800,000
(c)	For the extension and improvement of the network of functioning kindergartens by means of utilising and transforming into kindergartens new sites, porches and other light types of buildings in existing kindergartens, and small repairs to buildings taken over	30,000,000
	Total	46,800,000

On training cadres:

(a)	For training midwives and nurses of the People's Commissariat of Health	15,000,000
(b)	For teachers for town kindergartens of the People's Commissariat of Education	17,000,000
(c)	For preparation of teachers for village kindergartens of the People's Commissariat of Education	18,000,000
	Total	50,000,000

* After taking into account an 11 per cent decrease in construction costs.

APPENDIX

24. To assign 70,500,000 roubles for increased maternity aid in accordance with Pars. 5, 6, and 8 of this decision.

25. The Council of People's Commissars of the U.S.S.R. to guarantee the necessary materials for the projected construction in order that the People's Commissariats can begin construction by July 1 of this year.

26. To amend, for the purpose of establishing a uniform fixed system of financing kindergartens and children's nurseries, the decision of the Council of People's Commissars of the U.S.S.R. of July 6, 1935 (Code of Laws No. 35, 1935, Par. 310), " On obligatory dues of undertakings and institutions for the maintenance of children's nurseries and kindergartens," to one-quarter of one per cent of the wage fund, to fix direct allocations of 300,000,000 roubles for 1936 for this purpose from the State budget, and to make the corresponding changes in the finance plans of the economic organs and institutions, and also in the income and expenditure sides of the State social insurance budget.

VIII

ON MORE SEVERE PENALTY FOR NON-PAYMENT OF ALIMONY AND ALTERATIONS IN THE LEGISLATION ON DIVORCE

27. To amend the existing laws on marriage, family, and guardianship, with the aim of combating light-

APPENDIX

minded attitudes toward the family and family obligations, and to introduce in divorce proceedings the personal attendance at Z.A.G.S. (Civil Registry Bureau) of both divorcees and the entry into the passports of the divorcees of the fact of divorce.

28. To increase the fees for registration of divorce as follows: 50 roubles for the first divorce, 150 roubles for the second, and 300 roubles each for the third and subsequent divorces.

29. To allot in court judgment on alimony one-fourth of the wages of the defendant for the maintenance of one child; one-third for the maintenance of two children; and 50 per cent of the wages of the defendant for the maintenance of three or more children.

30. Payments to collective farm women to be made in workdays on the same basis.

If the mother receiving alimony is a collective farm woman and works with the defendant on the same collective farm, the management of the collective farm in calculating the workdays shall directly enter the corresponding share of the workdays earned by the father (if there are children) to the account of the mother. If the mother works on another collective farm, this entry in favour of the mother of the corresponding share of the workdays earned by the father shall be deducted on behalf of the mother in the final accounting of the workdays, by the management of the collective farm where the father works.

31. To raise to two years' imprisonment the penalty for non-payment of funds awarded by court for the

APPENDIX

maintenance of children, the search for persons refusing to pay alimony to be made at their expense.

M. Kalinin
Chairman of the Central Executive Committee of the U.S.S.R.

V. Molotov
Chairman of the Council of People's Commissars of the U.S.S.R.

I. Unschlicht
Acting Secretary of the Central Executive Committee of the U.S.S.R.

June 27, 1936.
Kremlin, Moscow.

INDEX

INDEX

ABIDOVA, Djakhan, 140
Abortions, decree prohibiting, 23–4, 254, 261–5
Academy of Science of the U.S.S.R., 134
Accountancy, employment of women, 31, 126
Adigea, illiteracy liquidated, 234
Administration, employment of women, 1935, 36, 37, 38, 121, 250
Agamirova, air pilot, 218
Agricultural machinery, employment of women, 62, 64, 65, 77–8
Agricultural schools, 70
Agriculture, employment of women, 38, 44 *et seq.*, 89 *et seq.*, 127; success of women in, 57; women in colleges, 124; women specialists, 132; artel, 208; and women in national republics, 233, 240 *et seq.*
Agronomists, women, 121, 125, 132
Agroskina, factory director, 137
Air defence, by women, 216–7
Alimony, penalties for non-payment, 12–13, 275–6
Ali Vairamova Club, 229
All-Donets competition for tractor-drivers, 101
All-Ukrainian competition for tractor-drivers, 101
All-Union Central Executive Committee, 96
All-Union Conference of Collective Farm Shock-workers, 20, 109
All-Union Congress of Soviets, women representatives at, 212
All-Union Engineers' roll of honour, 131
America, and Soviet woman engineer, 244–5
Angelina, Pasha, organiser of women's tractor-brigades, 100–1
Anna Karenina, by Tolstoy, 200
Anyshenok-Seglin, in army, 215
Aretunova, Arusya, engineer, 244–5
Armenia, women workers in, 231 *et seq.*
Army, women as officers, 220–1
Arzamas district, standard of living, 185
Askerova, air pilot, 218
Aviation, women engaged in, 217
Azerbaidzhan, cotton production, 104, 242; liberation of women, 228; women's conferences, 229; women workers in, 231 *et seq.*
Azov-Black Sea district, tractor-drivers in, 94

BABAEVA, FATIMA, oil worker, 240
Babushkina, N., parachutist, 218
Bach, N., research scientist, 135
Bairam-Ali district, cotton-growing, 243
Bakhbid, Ogul Guzel, shock-worker, 243
Baku, 239
Baku Aero Club, 218
Baranova, N., crack shot, 220
Barondina, V. M., tractor mechanic, 95–6
Bartseva, M., parachutist, 218
Bashkiria, crèche development, 148; liberation of women, 228; women workers in, 231 *et seq.*
Bath houses, 176
Bereznikov Chemical Combinat, 176
Bicycles, 184
Birth-rate, 169
Black Soil Regions, 89, 90
Blokhina, C., parachutist, 218
Bobriki, 83
Bolshoi Shuisky textile factory, 137
Book-keepers, women, 126, 133
Bootmaking, employment of women, 31, 62
Bragina, Vera, Order of Banner of Labour, 83
Brigadier, status on collective farm, 106–7
Buikova, record holder (sports), 188
Buikova, Claudia, Order of Lenin, 83–4
Building, employment of women, 36, 37, 38, 39, 66–7; Stakhanovite workers, 86
Buriat-Mongolia, girls in schools, 237
Burstein, R., research scientist, 135
Bykhovskaya, A., zoologist and biologist, 136

CALIBRE FACTORY, 245
Campaign of the five-hundreders, 57, 98, 208
Camps, holiday, 158
Cattle-breeding, employment of women, 57–8
Caucasus, shock-workers, 97; women's climbing expeditions, 187
Central Administration of National Economy Statistics, 136
Central Executive Committee, and employment of women, 60
Central Institute of Labour, Uzbekistan, 238
Chadra, the, 226
Chapayer division, 215
Chauffeurs, women as, 68
Cheliabinsk, crèches and kindergartens, 147, 155

INDEX

Chemical industries, employment of women, 31, 40, 41, 175-6; in national republics, 233
Chess, 186
Child-bearing, protection of women workers during, 19 *et seq.*
Child welfare, 22 *et seq.*
Children, parents' responsibility for, 12-13; education and employment of, 68 *et seq.*; of collective farm workers, 91; communal education, 144; medical services for, 149-50; extra-school work and services, 157-8; physique of, 1885-1934, 178-9. *See also* Crèche and Kindergarten
Church, and marriage in Tsarist Russia, 10; in U.S.S.R., 12
Chuvash Autonomous Province, 222-3; women workers in, 232; illiteracy in, 234
Circassians, illiteracy among, 234
Clubs, 196 *et seq.*; development of, in Soviet, 112; in Soviet East, 228; in national republics, 235-6
Coal-mining, employment of women, 73, 80; Stakhanovite movement, 56, and *see* Mining
Code of Labour Laws, 259-77
Coefficient, speed, of male and female labour, 74 *et seq.*
Collective farms, protection of women workers, 20; children's institutions, 154 *et seq.*; cultural level of women, 200-1; in national republics, 233; cotton, 242; crèches and kindergartens, 253
Collectivisation, 45 *et seq.*, 87-116
Combine drivers, women, 91, 93, 102 *et seq.*
Commerce, employment of women, 1935, 36, 37, 38
Communal services, 141 *et seq.*, 163 *et seq.*; in national republics, 246 *et seq.*
Communist Party, women's work in, 212 *et seq.*; in national republics, 249-50
Confectionery, employment of women, 128
Congress of Collective Farm Shock-workers, 99, 100
Consultation clinics, 149-50
Cooks, employed in field kitchens, 92
Co-operatives, employment of women, 44; importance of, 208
Cotton-growing, Stakhanovite movement, 57; production in Soviet, 104; in Eastern republics, 242 *et seq.*
Cotton industry, employment of women, 41, 62, 66, 73, 128; crèche organisation, 147; women in trade union, 203
Council of People's Commissars, on women in industry, 142-3; decree for liquidation of illiteracy, 192-3
Crèches, importance and organisation of, 142 *et seq.*; types of, 148-9; growth of, 253; in national republics, 247
Crimea, 102; kindergartens, 155; women workers in, 232; girls in schools, 237

DAGHESTAN REPUBLIC, women workers in 232 *et seq.*

Dead Souls, by Gogol, 200
Death-rate statistics, 177
Defence, women's work for, 214 *et seq.*
Demchenko, Maria, 57; initiator of " five hundred " campaign, 98-100
Denisova, Stakhanovite spinner, 86
Divorce, in Tsarist Russia, 10; in U.S.S.R., 12 *et seq.*
Dniepropetrovsk district, 102
Doctors, women, in Tsarist Russia, 119-20; 1931-5, 132; in national republics, 246
Domestic service, employment of women, 37-9
Domestic work, women released from, 142
Don Basin, housing improvements, 182
Donetz district, housing conditions, 183-4
Dorogomilov chemical factory, 130
Dowry, non-existent in U.S.S.R., 11
Draughtsmen, employment of women, 125-6
Dvinoles, timber vessel, 130
Dyachenko, skier, 187
Dzerzhinsky Metallurgical Factory, Ukraine, 205, 206

ECONOMY, National, women specialists, 1928-33, 122
Education; employment of women, 1935, 36, 37, 38; among collective farm-workers, 111 *et seq.*; women in colleges, etc., 123 *et seq.*; communal, of infants, 144; pre-school, 151; a " necessity," 195; workers' study circles, 197-8; in the republics, 228; *see also* crèches, kindergartens, factory schools
Egorova, Stakhanovite spinner, 86
Electrical industry, employment of women, 64, 65
Electrocombinat, Moscow, factory school of, 71, 131
Electrozavod factory (Moscow), productivity of women's labour, 74-5, 76, 81
Endineeva, milk maid, 241
Engineering, electrical, employment of women, 63; factory schools, 69
Engineering, technical, employment of women, 126
Engineers, women, 1933-5, 122-3
Entertainment (cinemas, etc.), 199, 201
Erisman, health survey, 1885, 178
Eugene Onegin, by Pushkin, 200
Examinations, for workers in heavy industry, 72 *et seq.*
Exportles, timber vessel, 130

FACTORIES, sanitary and technical conditions, 16
Factory schools, 33, 68 *et seq.*, 237
Fadeeva, E., weaver, 56
Families, help for large, 265-6
Family life, 255-6
Fedorova, E., knitting machine operator, 56; Vera, parachutist, 218
Field sports, 186

INDEX

Fighter machine-building factory, Moscow, 79, 80
Finance, for maternity homes, etc., 273-5
Five-hundreders, campaign of, 57, 98, 100, 208
Five-Year Plan, First and Second, 33 *et seq.*; material and cultural results, 49; factory schools, 68 *et seq.*; and higher education of women, 122 *et seq.*; development of crèche system, 145-6; development of kindergartens, 152 *et seq.*; house construction under, 181-2; women's social and cultural advance, 191 *et seq.*; and women of Mohammedan republics, 230
Flax production, Stakhanovite movement, 102
Fomina, live-stock farmer, 109
Food industry, employment of women, 31, 36, 37, 38, 41; communal services, 163 *et seq.*
Ford factory, America, 244
Franchise, women voters, 208-10, 250
Fur trade, employment of women, 41

GADJYAEVA, M. Y., Stakhanovite milkmaid, 104
Georgevsky district, 194; children's institutions, 156-7; communal laundries, 167
Georgia, women's conferences, 229; women workers in, 231 *et seq.*
German Volga Republic, 105
Gipromez (State Institute for Planning Metallurgical Factories), 135
Gliders, women, 219
Glukhov, physique of children, 1885-1934, 178-9
Gogol, 200
Golovchenko, Fekla, 194-5
Gorky, 200
Gorky district, kindergartens in, 155; standard of living, 185
Gorlovka, housing improvements, 182
Gramophones and records, 184
Gravilova, S., Red Cross organiser, 222-3
Grinstein, Sophie, shipbuilding engineer, 130
Grishina, A. H., manager of pig farm, 109-10
Guskova, Stakhanovite weaver, 86
Gymnastics, 186

HAMMER AND SICKLE FACTORY, Kharkov, 75, 76
Health, 141-90
Home of Mother and Child, 151
Houses, large scale production, 181-2

ILEYCH BAY COMPRESSOR GROUP, Baku, 239
Illarionova, E., Stakhanovite weaver, 85
Illegitimacy, in Tsarist Russia, 10
Illiteracy, liquidation of, 191 *et seq.*; in national republics, 234 *et seq.*

Ilyich factory, Kharkov, 205
Income, family, improvement in, 1929-35, 183
Industrial machinery, employment of women, 64
Industrial poisoning, 180
Industry, women drawn into, 14 *et seq.*, 38, 39, 51; women in colleges, 124; women specialists, 126, 127-8; in national republics, 233
Industry, heavy, employment of women, 40, 42, 61; factory schools, 69
Infant homes, 151
Infant mortality, 178
Ingushetia, illiteracy conquered, 234
Insurance, social, 17-19, 21-2; for children, 159-60; health statistics, 179-80
Inventors, women, 131 *et seq.*
Irdugan, skier, 187
Ivanova, skilled worker, 82
Ivanovo, crèche development, 149
Ivanov Province, kindergartens, 155

JANUARY UPRISING FACTORY, Odessa, men and women workers, 78
Jdanovich, 223
Jemchuzhnina, director of Teje Trust, 139
Jernov machine and tractor station, 102
Jordania, O., air pilot, 218

KABAKOVSK, 147
Kabardino, illiteracy, 234
Kaganovich bearing-factory, instruction of women, 72
Kalacheyev district, 150
Kalinin, M., 277
Kalinin collective farm, 223
Kalinin district, flax production, 103
Kaminsky, G., People's Commissar for Health, 150; on health services, 168-9
Kamneva, Nina, parachutist, 218
Karakalpakia, cotton-growing, 104, 242
Karelia, lying-in facilities, 170
Karl Marx factory, skilled women workers, 77, 79, 80
Karnenko, Professor, and "five hundreders," 100
Karpov Chemical Research Institute, 135
Kauchuk factory, Moscow, 131
Kazakstan, Stakhanovite movement, 57; women workers in, 231, 238; cotton growing, 104, 242
Kazan, 129; women's education at, 118
Kazan Flax Combinat, 240
Kazan fur factory, 240
Kazan sewing factory, 245
Kharkov, women's education in, 118
Kharkov electro-machine building factory, 75
Kharkov railway engine factory, 130
Kharlanova, Stakhanovite pig-breeder, 105
Khmelnitskaya, engineer production organiser, 130
Kholmogorsk, 109

INDEX

Kholmogorsk Soviet cattle farm, 105
Kidnapping, 249
Kiev, women's education at, 118
Kiev district, shock-workers, 97-8
Kindergartens, 143, 151 *et seq.*; in national republics, 247; growth of, 253; extension of, 270-2; supervision of, 272-3
Kirghizia, liberation of women, 228; women workers in, 232 *et seq.*
Kirov district, 109
Klinbergen machine, 129-30
Kloputunova, skilled technician, 129
Knitting industry, employment of women, 44, 128; women in trade union, 203
Kochenogova, factory director, 137-8
Kokorina, Z., air pilot, 217
Kolomensk machine-building factory, employment of women, 54, 71
Komiles, timber vessel, 130
Komsodi, school committees, 162
Komsomol, 83, 213; in national republics, 249-50
Koserev, P., inventor, 131
Kosheva, Anna, five-hundred, 99
Kostroma Linen Trust, 138
Kozieva, air pilot, 218
Kozub, Maria, Stakhanovite combine-driver, 102
Krasnii Textilshchiki, cotton factory, 137-8
Krasnokholmsky factory, Moscow, 137
Krauberger, E., Stakhanovite milkmaid, 104-5
Krivoi Rog Metallurgical Plant, 204
Krupskaya, No. 3, factory, Kazan, 137
Kuibishev district, crèche development, 148
Kulaks, liquidation of, 45
Kusina, engineer, 131
Kutalova, Tamara, parachutist, 219
Kuznetsova, record-holder (sports), 188

LABORATORIES, women workers, 128
Labour, hours of work, 16-17; employment of women, 18-19; fundamental tenet, 55; change of place of, for men and women, 80-1
Laundries, communal, 166-7
Law, employment of women, 121, 125
Leather work, employment of women, 31, 41
Lenin, V. I., attitude to women's life and work, 9; on organising talent of women, 111; and illiteracy, 192-3
Leningrad, instruction of women workers, 72; crèche development, 149; women defence workers, 216
Leningrad Institute for Organisation of Labour and Protection of Workers' Health, 176
Leningrad, Marti shipbuilding factory, 130
Leningrad province, kindergartens in, 155
Leninism, by Stalin, 53, 181
Lenjet Trust, 138-9
Levina, G., research scientist, 135
Levitina, engineer, 131

Literature, 199-200
Livestock farming, employment of women, 96 *et seq.*, 104-5, 241
Lukashova, Stakhanovite weaver, 86
Lunina, O., inventor, 131
Lying-in services, 170 *et seq.*, 248, 253-4

MACHINE BUILDING, Stakhanovite movement, 56; employment of women, 63, 73, 78; factory schools, 69; crèche organisation, 147
Magistrates, women, 133
Magnitogorsk, 147
Makeev Institute, investigation on employment of women in coal industry, 80
Malinovskaya, M., parachutist, 218
Manayenkova, M. C., social worker, 206
Marriage, position of wife in Tsarist Russia, 10, 11; in U.S.S.R., 11 *et seq.*; raising of age in republics, 248-9
Marshak, F., research scientist, 135
Marx, Karl, mathematical manuscript, 135-6
Maslova, record-holder (sports), 188
Master-shots, 220
Maternity aid, 169 *et seq.*
Maternity homes, extension of, 266-8
Maternity, law for protection of, June 1936, 22-5
Mechanisation, in heavy industries, 35-6
Medical institutions, 1917-35, 172
Medicine, employment of women, 31; women specialists, 1928-33, 122; women in training, 124
Metallurgy (Metal Industries), employment of women, 31, 40, 41, 42, 61-3, 65, 71, 73, 80; factory schools, 69; crèche organisation, 147; in Tartar republic, 233
Mikoyan, A., People's Commissar for food industry, 166
Military Academy of Mechanisation and Motorisation, 221
Military Engineering Academy, 221
Milk, yields under Stakhanovite movement, 104
Milling-cutters, employment of women as, 64, 71, 77-8
Milonova, industrial worker, 239
Minders of machines, employment of women as, 64, 65, 67
Mining, employment of women, 1913-26, 31, 40-41; crèche organisation, 147
Mining Academy, Moscow, 244
Miroshnichenko, record shot, 220
Mohammedanism, women's struggle against, 229-30
Molotov, V., 277; on cotton harvests, 104; on women voters, 209-10
Molotova, T., factory director, 137
Molyakova, Stakhanovite flax worker, 103
Mordovia, women workers in, 232
Moscow, women teachers and medical workers, 121; kindergartens, 155; communal food services, 163-4; lying-in facilities, 170; infant mortality, 178

INDEX

Moscow High School, 118
Moscow Metropolitan Railway (Metro.), 86
Mother, by Gorky, 200
Motor cars and tractors, employment of women, 63, 65

NABAT, GUL, shock-worker, 243
Nadeinskaya, E. P., specialist medal worker, 129-30
Nadezhdinsk, 147
Nartova, Katherine, Stakhanovite livestock farmer, 104
Nasurdinova, Hesny, technician constructor, 129
National Republics, women in, 224-51
Neidorf machine and tractor station, 102
Nelsina, E. I., military nurse and car driver, 215
New Economic Policy, 1921, 29 *et seq.*
Newspapers, women's work for, 198-9
Nikanorova, inventor, 131
Nikolayeva, A., parachutist, 218
Nogin factory, Vichuga, 84
Nurseries, extension of, 268-70
Nursing, employment of women, 31, 221

OCTOBER REVOLUTION, 214
October Revolution factory, Odessa, 79 80, 85; factory schools, 33
Octobrist Camps, 158
Odessa, women's education in, 118
Odintzova, T., weaver, 56, 85
Office staffs, employment of women, 31
Oil industry, employment of women, 80
On Beet Farming, by Prof. Karnenko, 100
Order of Lenin, 56, 84, 132, 218, 242
Order of the Red Banner of Labour, 56, 83, 137, 206, 215, 240, 242-3
Order of the Red Star, 218, 219
Order of the Sign of Honour, 207, 243
Ordjonikidze Oil Works, Baku, 243
Orekhovo Soviet grain farm, 102
Orgametal concern, 129
Orlovsky machine and tractor station, 111
Osoaviakhim, 222
Osoaviakhim circles and camps, 216-7

PAPER TRADES, employment of women, 1913-26, 31, 41, 66
Parachutists, women, 219
Parandja, the, 226, 249
Path to Lenin farm, 110
Pavlova, Stakhanovite weaver, 86
Peasants, and collectivisation, 45 *et seq.*, 87 *et seq.*
Pedagogics, women specialists, 1928-33, 122; women in training, 124; women in advanced, 134-5
People's Commissariat for Agriculture, Kazakstan, 238

People's Commissariat for Heavy Industries, 72
People's Commissariat for Light Industry, 128
People's Commissariats, employment of women, 138 *et seq.*
People's Courts, women's work in, 211
Perfumes and cosmetics, 138-9
Pergaments, C., chemist, 130
Persiantseva, Nadezhda, Stakhanovite livestock farmer, 104
Petrova, Maria, Stakhanovite combine-driver, 102
Physical culture movement, 187
Physique, of children, 1885-1934, 178-9
Pig-breeding, Stakhanovite movement, 105
Pirozhkova, Alexandra, Stakhanovite combine-driver, 102
Plasterers, women as, 67
Polishers, employment of women as, 64
Politics, women's rights in, 14-15
Printing trades, employment of women, 67
Prokopyeva, Tasya, Stakhanovite milk-maid, 105
Proletarskaya, inventor, 131
Prostitution, cessation of, 47
Public institutions, employment of women, 1935, 36
Public services, under Five-Year Plans 183
Pushkin, 200
Pyasetskaya, Galya, parachutist, 219

RABFAKS (workers' schools), 112, 121, 123-4, 196
Radenskaya, glider, 219
Radjalova, Vegil, organiser sewing artel, 245
Ragimova, Kemar, engineer, 243-4
Railway and transport, employment of women, 31, 67, 81
Rasogina, Stakhanovite flax worker, 103
Reading-huts, in national republics, 236
Reading-rooms, 197
Red Banner of Labour, 132, 245
Red Cross units, 221
Red Dawn collective farm, 104
Red Guards, 215
Red Half-Moon units, 221
Red October farm, 109
Red Profintern factory, 206
Red Putilov factory, 82
Research, on productivity of women's labour, 73-4
Research Institute for Mathematics and Mechanics, 135
Research, scientific, women engaged in, 134 *et seq.*
Rest homes, 173
Rion Hydro-Electric Station, 218
Rizhik, Raisa, in army, 216
Rodnikov Bolshevik Combinat, 85
Romanova, fur dresser, 240
Romanova, record-holder (sports), 188

INDEX

Roosevelt, President, 139
Rostov Agricultural Machinery factory, skilled women workers, 77–8
Rubber goods, employment of women, 128
Russia, Tsarist, position of women, 9–10; employment of women, 26 *et seq*, 42; position of peasant woman. 88–9; women workers in, 112–3; primary schools in, 112; higher education of women, 118, 119; infant education in, 152, 153; medical institutions, 172–3; death-rate, 177; sport in, 185–6; illiteracy in, 192; small nationalities in, 224 *et seq*.
Russian Socialist Federative Soviet Republic, 142–3

SAGANDINOVA, GASIZA, director of sewing factory, 245
Sagaoutdinova, G., factory director, 137
Salakhutdinova, weaver, 240
Saleswomen, 32
Sanatoria, 158
Saratov district, 102
Schools, factory, 68: on collective farms, 93; for illiterates, 193; for children, 195 *et seq*.; in national republics, 236 *et seq*.
Senturina, E. P., record shot, 220
Sewing trades, employment of women, 41, 44, 128; crèche organisation, 147; women in trade union, 203
Shakhnovskaya, skilled worker, 82
Shaposhnikova, director of Lenjet Trust, 139
Shengelia, Tugulia Egorovna, silk instructor, 240
Shishmareva, Anna, parachutist, 219
Shock-brigades, on collective farms, 91
Shock-workers, 55, 83, 97–8; in cotton farms of republics, 242–3; and social work, 202; *see also* Stakhanovite movement
Sholokhov, 200
Sholtz, Natalie, inventor, 131
Shooting, women's activities, 219–20
Shop managers, women, 126
Shvidka, Hannah, " five hundreder," 99
Siberia, kindergartens, 155
Sign of Honour Order, 56
Sitnikova, K. I., chairman of collective farm, 111
Smilga, A., director of Budget department, 139
Smirnova, E., deputy director Linen Trust, 138
Smirnova, T., deputy director Cotton Trust, 138
Social-economic services, women in training, 124
Socialism, ideals for women, 9
Socialism Victorious, 88
Socialist construction, women's part in, 137–8
Solbot, Alexandrovsk, machine and tractor station, 102
Solovyeva, M. A., of the Red Guards, 215

Soviet Union, principles underlying legislation affecting women, 9, 11 *et seq*.; labour laws, 16–17; social insurance, 17–18, 21–2; fundamental tenet on labour, 55; grades of workers (skilled, etc.), 61; laws for employment of women, 69–70; reorganisation of women's life, 141 *et seq*.; death-rate, 177; world sports records, 187, 188; nationalities of, 224; definition of, 226–7
Soviet Academy of Sciences, 134
Soviets, village, women elected to, 210–11
" Spartakiad," 187
Spas and sanatoria, 173 *et seq*.
Specialists, women, in industry, etc., 126 *et seq*.
Sport, development of, 185–90
Stakhanov, Alexei, 55
Stakhanovite movement, 55 *et seq*., 74, 84–6; on collective farms, 98; flax production under, 102–3; combine-drivers, 102 *et seq*.; wool-production, 104–5; live-stock, 104–5; milk-production, 104–5; pig-breeding, 105, 108; cattle-breeding, 108; effect on wages, 183; and women's cultural development, 192; and social work, 202; in national republics, 241
Stalin, Joseph, 82, 97, 156, 167, 194, 216; on peasant settlement, 53; on women on collective farms, 58; on rebuilding of the villages, 88; on women in collectivisation, 106; on modern worker's needs, 181; speech to Seventeenth Party Congress, 200; on importance of women, 214
Stalin district, cotton-growing, 243
Stalin factory (Moscow), 147; instruction of women, 72
Stalin Industrial Academy, 130
Stalin mine, 80
Stalinsk, crèche development, 148
State farms, employment of women, 115–6
State Planning Commission, on factory schools, 33; on communal food services, 164
Statisticians, women, 126, 136–7
Stein, S. I., social worker, 206
St. Petersburg High School, 118
Sukhina, S., Stakhanovite combine-driver, 102
Surovtseva, K. T., social worker, 206
Sverdlovsk, kindergartens, 155
Swimming, 186

TADJIKISTAN, Stakhanovite movement, 57; cotton production, 104; crèche system in, 146; women workers in, 231; cotton-growing, 242
Talovsky machine and tractor station, 95
Tarmantan, milkmaid, 241
Tartar republic, crèche development, 148; lying-in facilities, 171; women workers in, 231; illiteracy in, 234 *et seq*.

INDEX

Teachers, women, in Tsarist Russia, 119; higher education, 132–3; in national republics, 246
Technical schools, in national republics, 238–9
Technical workers, women, 121
Technicians, women, 122–3, 125
Teje Trust, 138–9
Telephones and telegraphs, employment of women, 67
Tennis, 186
Textile industries, employment of women, 31, 42, 44, 62, 66, 73, 82; Stakhanovite movement, 56; in national republics, 233
Tiflis Aero Club, 218
Tolstoy, 200
Towns, creation and planning of, 182–3
Tractors, number on collective farms, 92–3; women drivers, 94
Trade Unions, 202 *et seq.*; All-Union Central Council of, 51–2, 63; attitude to women workers, 58; and children's services and education, 159–60; oil workers, 239–40
Tram-conductors, women as, 68
Tram-drivers, women as, 68
Transcaucasian Socialist Federative Soviet Republic (Z.S.F.S.R.), crèche system in, 146
Transport, employment of women in, 31, 37, 38, 39, 67–8, 126–7
Trekhgorny textile factory, Moscow, 137; Stakhanovite spinners and weavers, 86
Tsvetmetzoloto State Research Institute, 135
Tula factory, 82
Tumen, 189
Turkmenistan, Stakhanovite movement, 57; crèche system in, 146; cotton production, 104; women workers in, 231 *et seq.*; cotton-growing, 242

UGOLKOVA, skier, 187
Ukolova, K., factory director, 137
Ukraine, housing improvements, 182; lying-in facilities, 171; marriage age, 248
Ukrainian Institute of Labour, 75
Ukrainskaya, V. A., chairman of collective farm, 110
Ulitina, skier, 187
Umova, C., engineer, 135
Unemployment, conquest of, 46–8
United States, average norm for combine-driver, 102
Universities, women engaged in, 1928–35, 123–4
Unschlicht, I., 277
Ural machine-building factory, 78; employment of women, 54
Uspensky machine and tractor station, 102
U.S.S.R. stratosphere balloon, 131
Utabaeva, milkmaid, 241

Uzbekistan, 140; Stakhanovite movement, 57; cotton production, 104; crèche system in, 146; women workers, 231 *et seq.*; cotton-growing, 242

VAGGINA, skier, 187
Vesnik, E. M., social worker, 204, 206
Village, organisation of, 112–3
Vinnik, Evdokia, Stakhanovite combine-driver, 102
Vinogradova, E., Stakhanovite weaver, 56, 84–5
Vinogradova, M., Stakhanovite weaver, 56, 85
Virgin Soil Upturned, by Sholokhov, 200
Vladimir Cotton Trust, 138
Volgales, timber vessel, 130
Volley-ball, 186
Volodarsky factory, Leningrad, 131
Vorobyeva, Anna, Stakhanovite flax worker, 103
Voronezh district, 150; women farm workers, 94; women in collective farms, 108
Voroshilov sharp-shooters, 219

WAGES, women's in Tsarist Russia, 26 *et seq.*; average family, 1929–35, 49
War, Great, position of women during, 27
Weaving, employment of women, 66; world record, 85
Welfare (health), employment of women, 1935, 36, 37, 38
White Russians, illiteracy of, 234
Women's Medical Institute, St. Petersburg, 118
Women, Soviet laws on rights and protection of, 9–25; position in Tsarist Russia, 9–10, 88–9; in industry, 14 *et seq.*; political rights of, 14–15; protection of workers, 15–16; payment for work, 17; protection during child-bearing, 19 *et seq.*; employment of, in Tsarist Russia, 26 *et seq.*; results of development of work for, 26–58; cultural level of, in Tsarist Russia, 27–8; in non-industrial occupations, 31–2; employment in Tsarist Russia and U.S.S.R., 32–3; importance of, in Five-Year Plan, 34–5; numbers employed, 1929–35, 36 *et seq.*; number and proportion of workers, 1929–35 (table), 38; material prosperity and health of, 43–4; increase of self-supporting, 50–1; social sources of workers, 51 *et seq.*; Stakhanovite movement, 56 *et seq.*; as skilled workers, 59–86; productivity of, in skilled labour, 73–4; desire to become literate, 73; earnings of, 81–2; Stakhanovite movement, 84; in collectivisation, 87–116; output of, on collective farms, 92; as tractor-drivers, 94; prejudice against, on collective farms, 94–5; time table of workers, 113–4; in intellectual and ad-

INDEX

Women—*continued*
ministrative work, 117–40; in special training schools, 123–4; in Government administrative posts, 139–40; employment in heavy work, 175; health of, in industry, 179–80; work and health relationship, 190; cultural growth and social activity, 191–223; liquidation of illiteracy, 191 *et seq.*; in trade unions, 202 *et seq.*; specialists' wives as social workers, 204–6; social activity in villages, 207; in co-operative stores, 208; in village soviets, 211; in People's Courts, 211; in defence, 215–6; in the national republics, 224–51; summary of activities, 252–6; work for, labour laws, 259–60
Wood-working, employment of women, 31, 41, 66, 80
Wool industry, crèche organisation, 147
Wool production, Stakhanovite movement, 105
Work-day, definition of, 92*n*.
World records, held by women, 188, 218 *et seq.*

YAKOLEVA, BARBARA, of People's Commissariat, 139
Yakovlev, on women in live-stock farming, 109
Yakovlev collective farm, 111
Yakovleva, O., parachutist, 218
Yanovskaya, professor of mathematics, 135–6
Yartsev factory, 73

ZHUKOVSKY AVIATION ACADEMY, 221
Zlatoust, 147